Royal Chitwan National Park
Wildlife Heritage of Nepal

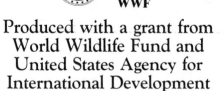

Produced with a grant from
World Wildlife Fund and
United States Agency for
International Development

Royal Chitwan
National Park
Wildlife Heritage of Nepal

Hemanta R. Mishra and
Margaret Jefferies

The Mountaineers
in association with
David Bateman

ROYAL CHITWAN NATIONAL PARK

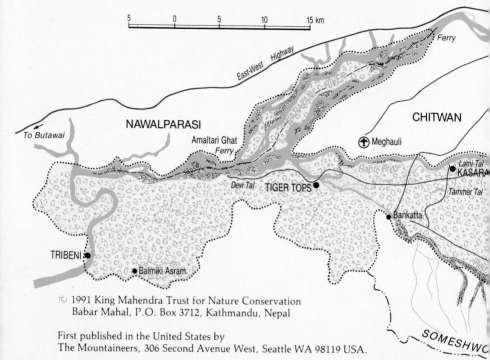

First published in the United States by
The Mountaineers, 306 Second Avenue West, Seattle WA 98119 USA.

The Mountaineers: Organized 1906 ". . . to explore, study, preserve and enjoy the
natural beauty . . ."

Address all trade enquiries to The Mountaineers (except India and Nepal to India
Book Distributors, 107/108, Arcadia, 195, Nariman Point, Bombay; Australia and
New Zealand to David Bateman Ltd, Auckland, New Zealand).

ISBN 0-89886-266-3

Published in association with
David Bateman Ltd., "Golden Heights", 32–34 View Road, Glenfield, Auckland,
New Zealand.

Designed by Pages Literary Pursuits, Auckland.
Printed and bound in Hong Kong by Colorcraft Ltd

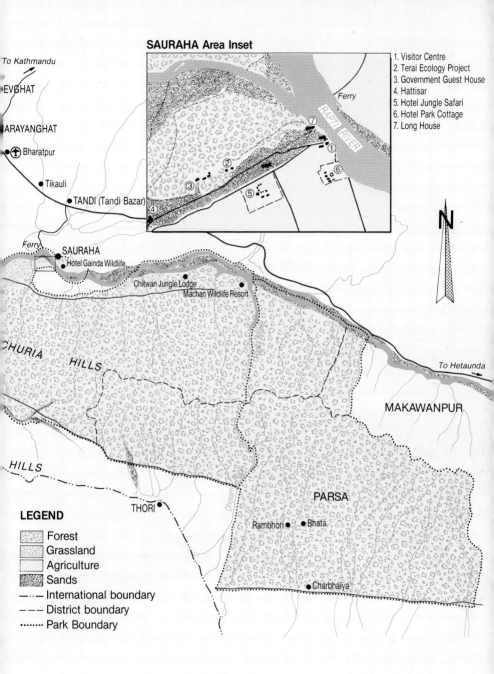

SAURAHA Area Inset

1. Visitor Centre
2. Terai Ecology Project
3. Government Guest House
4. Hattisar
5. Hotel Jungle Safari
6. Hotel Park Cottage
7. Long House

RAPTI RIVER

Ferry

To Kathmandu

EVGHAT

ARAYANGHAT

Bharatpur

Tikauli

TANDI (Tandi Bazar)

Ferry

SAURAHA

Hotel Gainda Wildlife

Chitwan Jungle Lodge

Machan Wildlife Resort

CHURIA HILLS

HILLS

THORI

Dhara

To Hetaunda

MAKAWANPUR

PARSA

Rambhori

Bhata

Charbhaiya

N

LEGEND

Forest
Grassland
Agriculture
Sands
—·—· International boundary
——— District boundary
········ Park Boundary

"Our land provides the visitor with a continual surprise of change and contrast, of richness and beauty. Its panoramic beauty has, since time immemorial, attracted sages and seers as it does attract modern explorers and tourists.

"We believe that there is a need for man to learn not only how to coexist in close bond with other men, but also in kinship with the birds, beasts and other animals with whom, in common, we inherit the earth. It is only through this coexistence that man will be able to realise not only the fullness and beauty and the infinite richness of the universe, but also the mystery, the harmony and order of creation, at all times."

His Majesty King Birendra Bir Bikram Shah Dev

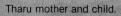
Tharu mother and child.

KING MAHENDRA TRUST FOR NATURE CONSERVATION

Patron　**HIS MAJESTY KING BIRENDRA BIR BIKRAM SHAH DEV**
Chairman　HIS ROYAL HIGHNESS PRINCE GYANENDRA BIR BIKRAM SHAH

MESSAGE FROM THE CHAIRMAN

A visit to the Royal Chitwan National Park is a unique experience. Outstanding for its rich flora and fauna, the Park remains today a preserve of an environment that is rapidly disappearing from our planet. This makes it one of the world's well known destinations, attracting several thousand visitors annually from all over the globe. Less than a century ago, much of Asia was like Chitwan, densely forested and teeming with wildlife. Today, except in a few protected areas, the remnants of vital ecosystems of bygone days can hardly be found. As we look at the world scene, we can only conclude that man has yet to learn to live in harmony with nature. Man's overuse of natural resources, without any thought to replenishing and sustaining them, is leading to the genesis of his own destruction. The importance of places like Chitwan lies in these thoughts. It is, indeed, in the fitness of things that the Royal Chitwan National Park has been designated as a World Heritage Site by the United Nations Educational Scientific and Cultural Organisation (UNESCO).

The publication of this book on the Royal Chitwan National Park helps illustrate Nepal's commitment towards conservation. It has been compiled to give you, the visitor, insight to the area's wildlife, as well as to the people who live on the fringes of the Park and the interaction that takes place between them. The coexistence and understanding of the complex relationship between Man and Nature is the only passage by which we can truly appreciate the need to protect our natural habitat, not as an isolated monument but in symphony with the overall interest of our people. Chitwan represents a living example of our endeavour in this direction. Your support is just as important in this effort. Learn to enjoy the Royal Chitwan National Park and leave it as you find it.

HIS ROYAL HIGHNESS PRINCE GYANENDRA BIR BIKRAM SHAH

NATIONAL PARKS BUILDING, BABAR MAHAL, P.O. BOX 3712, KATHMANDU, NEPAL
TELEX NP 2203 • CABLE NATRUST • TEL 215850 215912

Where more than one photograph appears on a page, references are from top to bottom in each column starting from the left column. **Johannes Bauer:** 15, 82, 86/1, 121/2, 123, 125/1/2/3, 141/1. **Diana Bell:** 46/1, 46/2. **Dept. of National Parks and Wildlife Conservation:** 23/3, 56/4. **Luke Golobitsh:** 60/1/2, 101, 114, 121/3. **Masahiro Iijima:** 2–3, 8–9, 10–11, 12–13, 16, 28, 31, 33/2, 37/1/2, 41/1/2, 42, 49, 49/3, 53, 56/1/2, 104, 107/2, 113/2, 126. **Bruce Jefferies:** 26, 77, 83/1/3, 85/2, 86/3, 90, 91/1/3, 96, 103/4, 105, 141/2. **Margaret Jefferies:** 56/1, 76, 91/2, 95, 129/1, 132, 136/1, 137, 139/1. **Hemanta Mishra:** 33/1, 33/3, 49/2, 62, 128. **Ulrike Muller-Boker:** 139/3. **Craig Potton:** 25, 44/1, 52, 56/3/5, 69, 80, 85/1, 87/1/3/4, 88, 93/1, 94/1, 107/4, 113/3, 117/4, 127, 135/1/2, 150, 156. **Fiona Sunquist:** 83/2, 148. **Balaram Thapa:** 37/3, 61/1/4, 87/2, 94/2, 97, 98, 103/2, 107/1, 110/4, 121/1/4. **Cecille Timmerman:** 93/2. **Pralad Yonzon:** 18, 61/3, 75. **Galen Rowell:** 110/5.

From the Tiger Tops Collection: **Devendra Basnet:** 61/5, 103/1, 110/1. **John Edwards:** 41/3, 117/1, 130. **Charles McDougal:** 30, 35, 39, 41/4, 45, 47, 61/2, 65, 68, 100/1, 102, 103/3, 110/6, 117/2/3, 119, 121/5. **Heldur Nectocny:** 4, 100/2, 139/2, 143. **Dieter and Mary Plage:** 110/2, 113/1. **Steve Power:** 107/3, 109. **Mike Price:** 66/2, 110/3. **Sanu:** 86/4. **John Wakefield:** 108. **Steve Webster:** 86/2.

Acknowledgements

Many people have assisted with the publication of this book, not only with photographs, information and helpful comments, but by making every visit to the Royal Chitwan National Park a memorable one. We would like to thank them all, especially the following: Biswa Upreti and the Department of National Parks and Wildlife Conservation; Lisa van Gruisen and the staff of Tiger Tops; the International Trust for Nature Conservation; Rajendra Lal Shrestha, Bhaya Kanal, Birendra Adhikari and Hemanta Ram Bhandary of the Natural History Museum for their help in identifying photographs; Drone Rajaure of Tribhuvan University; Colin Smith for up-to-date information on butterflies; the King Mahendra Trust for Nature Conservation.

P.B. Shah and staff of the Topographical Survey Branch of the Department of Survey provided diagrams and geological information; Dhruba Koirala drew the park map.

Historic photographs were provided by Kiran Mani Chitraker of Ganesh Photo Laboratory, Kathmandu.

Particular thanks and acknowledgement go to Gisele Krauskopf for her work and previously unpublished information on the Tharu. The information on plants used by the Tharu was generously given by Dr Ulrike Mueller-Boker.

Last, but not least, this book would not have been possible without funding from World Wildlife Fund US and the United States Agency for International Development, or the constant support and assistance of Bruce Jefferies, Chief Technical Advisor to the Department of National Parks and Wildlife Conservation 1986–9, who initiated the project.

Introduction

One hundred years ago the forests and grasslands of the Gangetic Plain stretched for thousands of kilometres. Lush, green and primeval, they were unbroken except for ribbons of water and scattered islands of tilled land.

The thrum of insects pervaded the pulsating heat. Chattering flocks of emerald parakeets played noisily from tree to tree while along river banks lapwings cried stridently, overriding the quiet cooing of doves and chittering of a host of other tiny forest birds. With brilliant wings flashing, butterflies bobbed and fluttered silently as they sought sustenance from flowers and moisture from damp patches of earth. Almost as quietly, the tiger, camouflaged by his black-striped tawny coat, slipped stealthily through the grasses, seeking shade in which to pass the heat of the day. Also seeking relief from the sun's beating rays, a rhinoceros settled his leathery grey bulk into the cooling waters of a muddy pool. Herds of elephants and wild cattle roamed freely, grazing the grasslands and browsing the forest greenery, while crocodiles basked log-like along river banks, absorbing the sun's warmth into their cold-blooded bodies.

As the crimson sank below a black silhouette of trees, cooler dusk temperatures drew deer from their shaded forest cover to feed in open grassy areas. Their spotted coats blending with the dappled light and shade of grasses and undergrowth, the chital grazed quietly until an intrusion sent them dashing noisily and swiftly for fresh cover. Safe once more they paused to turn and check the source of possible danger. Of calmer nature, the majestic sambar withdrew more quietly, vanishing into the concealing depths of dark foliage. In tree tops, the noisy crescendo as squabbling parakeets and mynahs settled for the night died away while the peacock's wail echoed mournfully over the darkening forest. A short staccato bark was answered by another, the call of barking deer, punctuating the quickening dark.

Young and still growing, the Himalayan mountain chain separates the cold, windswept plateau of the Tibetan Highlands from the sunbaked plains of India, and forms the spine of Nepal. But not all of Nepal's land is rugged and split by deep valleys.

Along the country's southern edge, where it borders with India, are the flatlands where valleys are broad and gentle. This is the Terai, a part of the Gangetic Plain. Averaging 150 m above sea level, the Terai is a tropical place where the fertile soil is nourished by huge rivers spilling out from the northern mountains. Each year, during monsoon floods, their waters overflow the flat plains, depositing new silt and bringing renewed life to the land.

Released from the narrow, confining gorges of the northern mountains, the
Narayani River spills broadly across the Chitwan Valley.

Vast areas of the Terai were once forested. Today remnants of those
forests are found only as small islands in a sea of agriculture. Royal
Chitwan National Park is one of these. Here wildlife still lives as it once
did throughout the Indian subcontinent. In the past, animals were
numerous everywhere and in little need of protection. Now many
species are extinct because of man's steadily increasing numbers and
underlying desire to dominate and control nature. Additional species are
threatened because their habitat is being destroyed by axes, ploughs, fire
and the grazing of domesticated animals.

Chitwan provides a haven for just over 300 of the world's 1000
greater one-horned rhinoceros (*Rhinoceros unicornis*). Although they
once ranged widely over the Indian plains, the only other place where
these rhinoceros survive in any numbers is Kaziranga National Park in
Assam, India. The Royal Bengal tiger is another threatened animal.
Around the beginning of this century there were an estimated 40,000
tigers in the world. Today that number is about 2000, mainly because of
habitat destruction. Even after strict legal protection only about 60
remain in the park area. They exist elsewhere in isolated areas of
western Nepal, but where their habitat is not protected they face
extinction.

A rhino enjoys a cooling wallow. Chitwan is a rare sanctuary for the endangered Asian one-horned rhinoceros.

The fish-eating Gharial crocodile, with a world population of less than 500 adults in the wild, has its greatest concentration in the section of Narayani River which flows through Royal Chitwan National Park. Even here they are threatened by overfishing, industrial effluent, river control and dams. The marsh mugger crocodile, mainly an inhabitant of marshes and lakes also numbers less than 100 in Chitwan, although there are an estimated 2000–3000 in India. How long will it be before the swamps and ponds vital to the mugger's survival are destroyed?

The list of threatened species grows steadily as more and more wildlife habitat is converted to agricultural land. Only by protecting what remains from the inundating and destructive tides of human interference is there any chance for this wildlife to survive.

Chitwan is unique. There are now few areas in the world which can match its variety and abundance of wildlife — a variety and abundance only possible because the dense forests and grasslands provide conditions and food necessary for the animals' survival. But it is not only wildlife that Chitwan contains. The flora, water, soil and insects which combine to create an environment suitable for animals are also important in maintaining the welfare of humans. The Park already has a proven value to the people who live near its boundaries. Some plant species of the Terai have now been collected to such an extent that they are difficult to find. Grass used for thatching the roofs of local houses has disappeared from land outside the National Park. It still flourishes in Chitwan, but only because of strict conservation measures.

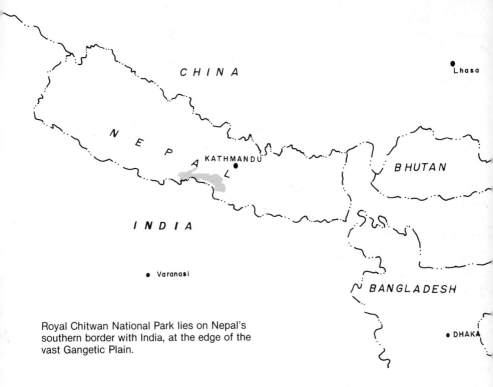

Royal Chitwan National Park lies on Nepal's southern border with India, at the edge of the vast Gangetic Plain.

Like a bank for the safe keeping of material valuables, this untouched wildland and its fauna form a repository of biological diversity. Within it are the plant and animal genes needed to ensure our own survival. In our search for better medicines and more productive strains of animals and plants we must look to wild species. So far, hundreds of wild plants and animals have been found to be useful. Thousands more have yet to be studied for their potential value. But, as time goes on and more wildlands are converted to agricultural land, they will only be found in protected areas such as national parks. Maintaining this enormous genetic resource for the future can only be done by ensuring that natural areas are adequately protected. Without them the world would be a much poorer place — one that could possibly be uninhabitable by us! We therefore have no choice — only a definite responsibility to preserve natural environments and their associated wildlife in the most unchanged state possible.

Chitwan has been accorded a special status to give it the protection it deserves. In recognition of its importance, not just to Nepal but to the whole world and all of mankind, Chitwan has been designated by the United Nations Educational, Scientific and Cultural Organisation (UNESCO) on behalf of the world community as a World Heritage Natural Site.

17

Following old hunting methods, white cloth is laid out in a "V" which will direct the tiger close to the researcher's tranquilliser gun.

1. The Human Invasion

A Sport for the Privileged

Before the 1950s the Terai forests were afforded some protection by the Rana rulers of Nepal, not because they were conservation-minded but in order to pursue their interest in the sport of big-game hunting. Tiger, rhinoceros, leopards and bears were all much more numerous then, and wildlife preservation was an unknown concept.

In 1846 the first Rana Prime Minister, Jung Bahadur Rana, declared the rhinoceros a royal game animal, giving it a measure of protection. Penalties imposed for poaching were severe and a definite deterrent. Large hunting parties, organised by the Ranas for their own pleasure and for visiting royalty or other dignitaries, were magnificent affairs. Held in the mosquito-free months of December to February, when temperatures were cooler, they lasted several days. Hundreds of elephants were used, gathered together from all over Nepal to help with transport and to locate and hunt the wildlife.

To shoot the elusive tiger, two main methods were used. In both, live buffalo calves were staked out at selected sites as bait. If the bait was taken, indicating the presence of a tiger, the surrounding area was encircled with a strip of white cloth, forming a metre-high wall. Outside the cloth stood a ring of elephants. Marksmen would enter the circle on elephants and shoot all the tigers and any other wildlife trapped within. Although the tigers had little hope of escape, they could hide temporarily in the long grasses, often for a considerable time before being caught, which gave the hunt an element of excitement.

In the other method, shooting was done from a *machan* — a hide constructed in the centre of the ring. Using a large number of elephants, the hunters pushed and manoeuvred the tiger towards the machan until it was close enough to provide a clear target.

Biologists conducting research on the tiger have adopted this traditional method for capturing and sedating the animal. Here they lay the white cloth, known locally as *vhit*, in a "V" shape, with the marksman, armed with a drug-loaded dart gun, hidden in a tree at the narrow end of the funnel. Then, shouting and thrashing the vegetation, men and elephants move steadily from the wide end, driving the tiger before them toward the marksman. Despite being more than capable of jumping over the thin barrier and escaping, either instinct or fear forces the tiger to avoid the white cloth.

Success of a hunt was invariably measured by the number of animals killed: 39 tigers, 18 rhinos, 4 sloth bears and several leopards was the tally during one organised for the visit of King George V of England in

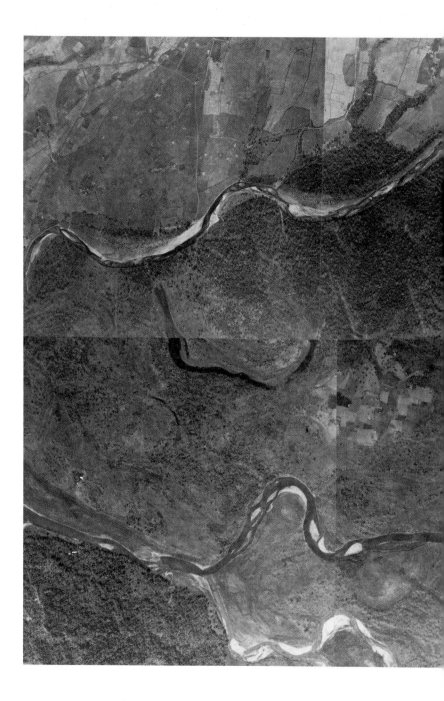

The western end of the Park between the Rapti and Reu rivers. The numerous illegal settlements within the Park in 1963 show clearly in the lower half of the photo. These have since reverted to grassland.

1911. This record was broken in 1938-9 during a hunt in which Lord Linlithgow, Viceroy of India, took part. A total of 120 tigers, 38 rhinos, 27 leopards and 15 bears were taken. In comparison, Jung Bahadur Rana's kill of 21 elephants, 31 tigers, 3 leopards, 1 rhino, 7 sambar stags, 20 other deer, 1 crocodile, 4 bears and 6 pheasants in 1850 was small.

With tallies such as these, several years were needed for the animals to recoup their numbers. Fortunately, as hunts were only held irregularly and in different areas each time, the effect on total wildlife populations was not too devastating. Also, the high quality and amount of suitable habitat remained untouched, providing optimal conditions for animals to breed undisturbed.

The Jungle Barrier

The Terai jungles and grasslands presented a natural barrier and great deterrent to anyone wishing to enter Nepal, whether peacefully or forcefully, and helped to keep the country isolated from the rest of the world. With a deliberate policy of maintaining these forests as a barrier against invasion from the British Empire in the south, the Rana rulers prohibited cultivation in the Rapti Valley during the early 19th century. This was not particularly difficult to enforce, for the Terai was not an attractive place to live. A torrid summer climate and extensive wet areas

Rhino hunts were a sport reserved for the Rana rulers and visiting royalty.

Skins of poached rhinos retrieved by Park staff, 1974.

23

within the jungle and grasslands provided breeding grounds for mosquitoes which carried a deadly type of malaria. Fearing this disease, hill people avoided the Terai, but it was inhabited by a few other tribal groups.

A Barrier Broken

With the downfall of the Rana regime in 1950 came many changes. The protection previously afforded to wildlife and habitat, and viewed as another form of Rana oppression, was now removed. Due to the political instability, poaching and deforestation increased dramatically.

Rhino are still poached, mainly for their horns which fetch high prices in eastern Asia for their supposed medicinal properties. Powdered rhino horn derived from the Asian species is considered superior to that from the African species. In the Yemen Arab Republic a dramatic increase in the use of rhino horn for making the handles of traditional daggers, owned by almost all adult males, has led to the slaughter of African rhinos. Although the Nepalese revere the rhino, this has not stopped them from killing it, as almost every part of its anatomy is considered useful.

Poaching is not the only problem. A lack of arable land and an ever-expanding population in the hills led the government to launch a resettlement programme. As a result, many people came down from the hills to live in the Chitwan valley. To aid this resettlement, a malaria eradication programme, commenced in 1954 by the United States' Agency for International Development (USAID), rendered more land habitable by humans. By the time this programme ended in 1960, the 1950 population of 30,000 people in the Terai had expanded to 100,000. By then 65 per cent of Chitwan's forests had been cut to create agricultural land and provide timber and fodder, and much valuable wilderness was lost forever.

Preserving the Remnant

In 1961, with the commencement of political stability, many officials were concerned by the burgeoning population in the Terai and correspondingly low survival chances of the rhino and other species. An attempt was made to give some protection to the land and wildlife under a newly introduced Forest Act. Over 80,000 ha were set aside as Chitwan Rhinoceros Reserve, but this attempt was not successful as there were numerous settlements within prime rhino habitat.

In 1964 the Land Settlement Commission, set up by the Nepal government, looked into the legal status of Chitwan settlers and had

22,000 people removed and resettled elswhere. But the problem was still not solved. People living around the boundaries of the protected area continued to use the forests as a source of firewood and fodder, and the environment continued to decline, with a consequent fall in wildlife numbers. A 130-strong force of armed guards, called the *Gaida Gasti* or Rhino Patrol, had many clashes with poachers during their mounted patrols, but attained only limited success in curbing the poaching. By 1968 the number of rhino in Chitwan was estimated to have declined to about 100, and they were in danger of extinction unless completely protected. Tigers were also a rare sight. Other species such as swamp deer disappeared from Chitwan during the mid 1960s.

Establishment of a national park appeared to be the only way to protect the area and its wildlife. In December 1970 the late King Mahendra directed the government to create a national park in Chitwan. Legal status for Royal Chitwan National Park was provided in 1973, when the present sovereign of Nepal, His Majesty Bir Bikram Shah Dev, promulgated Nepal's first National Parks and Wildlife Conservation Act. This provided a legal status for the Royal Chitwan National Park.

Preliminary development of the Park was administered by the National Parks and Wildlife Conservation Office, a small unit of the Forest Department. With the addition of more protected areas

Headquarters for the Park are at Kasara, housed in an old hunting lodge.

throughout Nepal, a new Department of National Parks and Wildlife Conservation was formed in 1980. Law enforcement within all the national parks and wildlife reserves is the responsibility of the Royal Nepal Army.

Further action to provide larger areas and better habitat for tigers and other wildlife was taken in 1978 when the original area of Chitwan was extended to cover 932 sq km. A further 499 square kilometres adjoining the park's eastern boundary became Parsa Wildlife Reserve. By 1988 Parsa had been included within the boundaries of Royal Chitwan National Park.

The next important step came in December 1984. In recognition of its richness in flora and fauna, and representativeness of a primeval forest and grassland type which is fast disappearing from this earth, Chitwan was declared a World Heritage Natural Site by the United Nations Educational, Scientific and Cultural Organisation (UNESCO).

The Advent of Tourism

Tourism did not come to Chitwan with a big rush but has increased steadily from a slow beginning of a few hundred people per year in 1964

Tiger Tops Jungle Lodge, the oldest established accommodation within the Park.

to nearly 15,000 in 1988. At first, the only accommodation for tourists was a lodge at the western end of the Park, styled on African tourism concepts. Opened in 1964, the then modest four-bedroomed structure is the now well known Tiger Tops Jungle Lodge, which operates within the Park under an agreement with His Majesty's Government.

Under a similar agreement, Gaida Wildlife Camp opened in the early 1970s at Sauraha, about 36 km east of Tiger Tops. As early roads to the Terai were little more than rough tracks used by ox-carts, they were a discouragement to would-be visitors. With improvements to the east-west highway between Hetauda and Narayanghat and the opening of the highway between Mugling and Narayanghat, access to the area became much easier. Visitor numbers expanded accordingly, and since the beginning of the 1980s small, budget-type camps and lodges at Sauraha, where the Park entrance is located, have mushroomed to accommodate them.

The eastern end of the Park is also becoming more popular since two more licensed operations, Chitwan Jungle Lodge and Machan Wildlife Resort, opened in 1986 and 1987. Several more lodges are planned for other areas.

Leopards often climb leafy trees where the dappled light provides concealing cover.

2. Call of the Jungle

Ancestors

Fifty million years ago, when the Himalaya began to rise, a great variety of animals roamed the swamps and forests of the Indian subcontinent. Gradual climatic changes eventually made conditions unsuitable for their survival, causing many of them to disappear. Not only proof of their existence, but also their form and size are clearly visible to us as fossilised remains in rocks forming the upper layers of the Siwaliks.

Many of those animals — giraffes, eland, kudus, chimpanzees, baboons, hippopotami — are now found only in Africa. It is possible that they all shared the same ancestors, which may have originally migrated southward from Europe or Central Asia. These regions once enjoyed a more tropical climate, but with increasingly colder temperatures during the last ice age, beginning two million years ago, animals progressively migrated southward to warmer areas in order to survive.

Of the original 11 known species of elephant and mastodon, six species of rhinoceros and several types of wild boar present then, only one form of each exists in Chitwan today. The present form of rhinoceros is a close relative of *Rhinoceros unicornis fossilus*, a species which died out a million years ago. A massive four-horned ruminant, the *Sivatherium*, also existed then, but left no descendants.

Predators were also more numerous and included sabre-toothed tigers, cheetahs, and other cats. Mammals present today, the langurs, hyenas, jackals, foxes, sloth bears, ratels, and porcupines are similar to those which existed millions of years ago.

Eat And Be Eaten — a Law of The Wild

All the creatures living in an area such as Chitwan belong to an organised community. Although each lives a separate life within the same habitat, each one influences the lives of all the others. All exist in balance, each animal playing a particular role and contributing to the maintenance of the community as a whole. The relationships between members of the community centre mainly on food and its distribution.

Plants are the basic food of animals, and herbivores form the largest class in any community of mammals. The plant-eaters provide food for carnivores. Without herbivores, there would be no carnivores.

Then there are the scavengers, which live off the remains of other animals and help to keep the land clean. Even some predators will take

Hog deer are a leopard's favourite prey.

to scavenging if live prey is difficult to obtain. In addition, there are some omnivorous animals which eat both plants and flesh. At the bottom of the scale are the parasites, creatures which live off other animals. Basically, all animals depend on plants; without plants there would be no animals. Both day and night have their own set of hunters and hunted, scavengers and parasites — one of Nature's ways of minimising competition for food.

Each herbivore consumes different vegetation, ensuring that optimal use is made of the Park's food resources. For example, although hog deer and rhinos both prefer to graze grasslands, they do not compete for the same plants. Squirrels and monkeys are able to utilise flowers, fruit and nuts near the tops of trees. The fliers — fruit bats and birds — eat fruit that is out of reach of the squirrels and monkeys. Other rodents feed on seeds, roots, tubers, nuts, flowers and fruits nearer ground level.

Each carnivore provides a check on a particular herbivore or group of herbivores. The size and strength of the predator determines its particular herbivore prey. Some carnivores, however, such as wild dogs, hunt in packs and are able to kill animals much larger than themselves by their combined efforts and strength.

Tigers keep the larger herbivores — sambar, chital deer and wild cattle — in check. Not as powerful, the leopard is limited to controlling the smaller herbivores such as hog deer and barking deer, and therefore occupies a lower link in the food chain. The intermediate and smaller

Before eating, a tiger drags its prey into safe cover. Feeding starts at the rump and up to 30 kg of meat can be consumed in one meal, with a chital deer lasting two days.

cats, such as leopard cats, jungle cats and fishing cats, prey on even smaller herbivores — the hares and rodents.

Limiting factors for a large carnivore like the tiger are the conditions of cover within the area it inhabits. Its greatest enemy is Man, who kills wantonly and destroys the habitat, or other tigers, which compete for food. Leopards fear tigers. Likewise, lesser carnivores fear other bigger ones.

Usually the smallest animals are more numerous in any community because of their ability to increase their numbers easily. Generally, as the size of an animal increases the number of young it produces decreases, and the less successful it is at long-term survival.

The law of "eat and be eaten" applies not only to mammals but to all the creatures of Chitwan, whether they be insects, arachnids, molluscs, birds, reptiles, amphibians or fish.

The Hunters

The big cats

The **tiger** occupies the apex of the food pyramid and is the animal which captures our imagination the most. Known in the past as the Royal Bengal tiger (*Panthera tigris tigris*), this magnificent animal is the largest of all cats and undoubtedly king of the jungle. Once bold and having little fear of Man, the tiger has been hunted and killed extensively in the past. Today this animal is famous for its tenuous hold on life and for the international efforts, launched during the last two decades, which have been successful in bringing it back from the brink of extinction.

Some of these efforts include research to provide clues as to why this animal is more vulnerable and threatened than others. Five separate but related studies conducted in Chitwan between 1973 and 1981 have brought to light many interesting facts about tigers and their prey. During these studies a number of tigers were darted and tranquillised, then fitted with radio collars so that their movements could be followed. The tranquillising and capture were done in much the same way as the old tiger hunts were carried out.

A secretive, elusive creature, the tiger usually avoids humans where possible, and the chances of seeing one during a Park visit of only 2 or 3 days are slim. Sometimes visitors are lucky and are rewarded with more than just a glimpse. Occasionally, when rounding a bend in a road or trail, they may find one of these big cats just standing, staring back at them. Unless the tiger is a female with cubs, it will not usually attack. It is more likely to walk calmly away into the grasses or forest undergrowth, where its striped coat quickly renders it invisible.

Tigers are usually more active during late afternoon and at night, particularly during the hot dry season when movement of prey species is limited by the heat. In one night, individuals can cover over 20 km in search of food. During the day the tiger will occupy shaded resting-sites close to streams, lying on its side, belly or back, or else partially submerged in water.

Being territorial creatures, male tigers need an area as large as 50 to 60 square kilometres; females use between 25 and 30 square kilometres. A male's territory usually encompasses that of two to four females and it seems that this territorial behaviour is a means of spacing individuals to make the best use of food supplies without damaging its renewal potential.

Although humans are unaware of the whereabouts of tigers, except for their footprints, these wary cats do advertise their presence and mark their territory for the benefit of other tigers. As they patrol, moving along riverbanks, paths, trails or open areas which offer the easiest travel, they periodically scrape the ground with their hind paw, leaving a distinctive mark. A scat is often deposited on this mark. Urine sprayed on to trees, and claw marks on large tree trunks which lean over a trail, are other signs. The urine has a distinctive smell which lingers for some time and indicates to other tigers whether the owner is male or female, and its sexual condition.

Mating takes place in all seasons and after a gestation period of 15 to 16 weeks a litter of one to six cubs is born in a well protected site. The mortality rate among cubs is high during their first year of life and usually a tigress is successful in raising only one or two cubs per year, even though they are at times seen with more. Adult male tigers are known to kill male cubs, especially when they are trying to take over a new territory. The cubs are blind for their first 17 days and at birth are about the size of an adult domestic cat, weighing around 1.8 kg. They are nursed by their mother for about 6 months, then are gradually

(Left) Tracking a tiger with radio telemetry. (Right) A tiger marks its territory.

A tranquillised tiger is weighed, measured and fitted with a radio collar.

trained by her in hunting and killing techniques, normally becoming independent between 18 months and 2 years.

The sub-adult, now looking for a territory of its own, usually stays around the periphery of another tiger's territory, waiting for a chance to take it over. The alternative is to disperse from the natal area to adjacent localities where the habitat is not as good and survival chances are slimmer. For these reasons tigers need a lot of space and good habitat, and it seems that in Chitwan the breeding population of about 35-40 is about as many as the Park can accommodate.

The chances of sighting a **common leopard** (*Panthera pardus*) are slightly better as these cats are more active during daytime. Their black-spotted, tawny coats provide excellent camouflage, however, and they are often almost invisible even from a short distance.

Unlike tigers, leopards can thrive almost anywhere, utilising a great range of prey. Hunting is normally done at dusk and dawn, but if unsuccessful, leopards will continue their search during the day. They are solitary, territorial creatures like tigers, but have much smaller home ranges of 4–12 square kilometres. Ranges of males and females overlap, but those of the same sex do not. Leopards also use urine and scrape marks to mark boundaries and to indicate sexual condition.

Leopards can climb trees with amazing speed and agility, something tigers cannot do. Their strength is exceptional and they can drag their kill, often an animal heavier than they are, up into a tree so that it can be consumed without disturbance from other predators or scavengers. Like tigers, they also swim well.

Litters of three or four leopard cubs are born at any time of the year, after an 85-95 day gestation period. The young are blind for their first week, and extremely vocal until about 2 months old. Their drawn-out, rasping mew later changes to the grunting snarl, known as "sawing", emitted by mating adults.

The rarest of all cats, the **clouded leopard** (*Neofelis nebulosa*), is nocturnal and mainly arboreal, so is hardly ever seen. Although specimens have been caught in the Terai, the presence of this animal in Chitwan National Park has not been confirmed. Slightly smaller and lighter in build than the common leopard, the clouded leopard's colour varies from an earthy grey-brown to yellowish-brown with dark oval patches and pale underparts. Very large upper canine teeth enable it to kill deer and other large animals.

Small cats

The smallest felid in Chitwan, the **leopard cat** (*Felis bengalensis*) is even smaller than a domestic cat and measures only 1 m, including the long tail. This soft-furred, nocturnal predator is like a miniature of its big relative, the common leopard. A forest dweller, it prefers dense cover and thus is rarely seen.

The jungle cat's colouring blends well with the grassland where it prefers to hunt.

Jungle cats (*Felis chaus*) are seen more frequently because of their diurnal lifestyle and preference for grasslands and forest edges. Although measuring about the same length as leopard cats, they have much shorter tails and a heavier build. Their yellowish-grey coloured coats have darker stripes on the legs and on the black-tipped tail.

Fishing cats (*Felis viverrina*) are also relatively common, frequenting thick forests and swampy grass areas. Unlike other cats, the fishing cat's claws are not fully retractile. They do not enter the water to catch food, but lean down from banks or boulders and scoop up fish and molluscs with their web-toed forefeet. Adults measure about 1.25 m from nose to tail-tip and weigh 9-16 kg. Their tails are shortish, with dark rings, and their drab, grey-brown body-fur has rows of elongated dark spots which merge to form stripes on the back of the neck and head.

Foxes, jackals, dogs, and hyenas

Foxes, wild dogs, jackals and hyenas are all inhabitants of Chitwan, but each occupies a different niche. The **Indian fox** (*Vulpes bengalensis*) is quite common in open areas. Solitary, and small at less than 3 kg, this lithe grey animal has long limbs and a bushy, black-tipped tail. It hunts during the night for small animals and also eats insects and fruit. After a pregnancy of about 50 days, two to six cubs are born in a well concealed and protected burrow.

Jackals (*Canis aureus*) are also relatively common in the Park and adjacent farmlands, preferring grasslands to other environments.

Reaching 40 cm at the shoulder, their colour varies from pale yellowish through all shades of grey and brown. Four to six young are produced after a gestation period of about 2 months. At night, the jackals' strange, long drawn-out howling as they hunt for ground-roosting birds and small mammals is a disconcerting sound. They also scavenge, and are known to eat fallen fruit and to raid sugarcane and corn fields.

Although distributed throughout most of Asia right up to the treeline, the **wild dog** (*Cuon alpinus*) is an endangered species and is rare in Chitwan. Taller and heavier than jackals, their coats are usually a bright reddish-brown, and their tails longer and bushier, with a dark end. An adult can weigh up to 20 kg and can have a head and body measuring almost a metre in length. Probably the ancestor of domestic dogs, the wild dog differs by having only six molar teeth instead of seven on the lower jaw, and 12 to 14 nipples in contrast to the 10 possessed by true canids. Neither do they bark like domestic dogs. When hunting, the wild dog's call is a chorus of shrill chattering, and at other times a whistling sound.

Wild dogs are extremely efficient killers, hunting in small packs during the early morning and at dusk, chasing larger animals such as chital and sambar. They can run at 45 km per hour, eventually running down their prey, and have been known to challenge redoubtable rivals such as tigers and bears. As they are not scavengers, these dogs must hunt to survive. Being in a pack gives them a distinct advantage.

To advertise their presence to other dogs, they mark their path by dropping faeces at regular intervals, leaving behind a strong scent which also helps in sex identification. Usually from two to six young are born after a gestation period of 70 days. The pups are blind at birth and kept secure in caves or under rocks. After weaning they are fed regurgitated food until they are big enough to join the pack for hunting.

Preferring the open plains to the south, the **striped hyena** (*Hyaena hyaena*) does not often venture to the more confining vegetated areas of the Park in the north. This loathsome-looking scavenger is also an efficient predator, hunting in small groups and running down small ungulates and other animals. A dull, dirty yellow-grey coat, striped with black across the back, chest and legs, and a large head and powerful forequarters emphasise the hyena's rather mean appearance.

Other small carnivores
Mongooses
Slinking unobtrusively through shrubbery and across open ground, the **common mongoose** (*Herpestes edwardsi*) is well camouflaged by its greyish-brown grizzled fur. A lithe body on short legs provides the mongoose with incredible agility when dealing with snakes, a favourite food which it hunts in open forests. Birds, rodents, vegetable matter and occasionally carrion form the rest of its diet. Pregnancies are only 2

The reddish coat and bushy tail of the wild dog (right) distinguish it from the jackal (above). Mongooses (below) are formidable hunters of snakes.

months long, and, being prolific breeders, mongooses produce up to three litters a year. Young are born in holes under rocks or trees, or even chambers within old termite mounds.

The semi-aquatic **crab-eating mongoose** (*Herpestes urva*) is an expert swimmer and eats fish, crabs, frogs and molluscs. Although similar in size to the common mongoose, the crab-eating mongoose is more heavily built and has distinctive white stripes along the sides of its face and shoulders. Defence tactics are to squirt putrid-smelling liquid, from large anal glands, at any would-be attackers.

Mustelids

One of the more attractive predators of Chitwan's forests is the **yellow-throated marten** (*Martes flavigula*). Its slim, weasel-like body is dark brown, but middle parts are lighter and the throat and belly are a creamy-yellow. Martens hunt small rodents, birds and reptiles, usually working in pairs, often with one animal flushing the prey out for the other to catch by surprise. Another method is for both animals to chase prey until it becomes exhausted. Yellow-throated martens are found throughout Nepal, including in the high mountains.

The elusive **ratel** or **honey badger** (*Melivora capensis*) is another mustelid inhabiting the Park, but, being a nocturnal creature, its existence there remained unrecorded until only a few years ago. Ratels have elongated feet with non-retractile claws which are well adapted for digging out small prey from burrows. A long muzzle with a blunt snout and good olfactory powers also helps the animal to search out food efficiently.

Boldly marked in black and white, ratels are reputed to be fearless animals, probably because their defence mechanism is a putrid-smelling liquid produced by skin glands. Once contaminated by the stink, a predator cannot get rid of it for several days.

Civets

Civets are a group of small to medium-sized predators with pointed snouts, short legs, long bodies and tails. They bear a slight resemblance to cats. A secretion from the perineal glands of some species is used in the preparation of medicines and perfumes. Of the six species found in Nepal, four occur in Chitwan and all are nocturnal.

The **common palm civet** or **civet cat** (*Paradoxus hermaphroditus*) is dark grey with a black face, legs and tail-tip. Adults average a length of 1.2 m, including the tail. They prefer to live near villages where they can easily hunt rodents and poultry or raid crops. Litters of two to four young are born throughout the year.

Both large Indian and small Indian civets have greyish coats marked with rows of dark spots, and tails with black and white rings. The **large Indian civet** (*Vivvera zibetha*), which averages 1.2 m in length, including the tail, prefers forests where it hunts for birds, reptiles and small mammals. Fruit and roots are also eaten.

The **small Indian civet** (*Viverricula indica*) usually measures less than a metre. Like palm civets, small Indian civets prefer inhabited areas where they can hunt rodents and other small animals, and obtain fruits and vegetables easily. Litters of three to five young are born in burrows throughout the year.

Rarely seen in Chitwan, the **tiger civet** or **spotted linsang** (*Prionodon pardicolor*) is a handsome animal with a black-spotted, tawny-yellow coat. A long, black and white ringed tail forms almost half the animal's

Many animals, such as the civet cat, are only active at night, so are rarely seen.

total length of about 75 cm. Small animals and birds, both terrestrial and arboreal, are the tiger civet's main diet. Unlike the other civets, it does not possess scent glands.

The Hunted

Ungulates

The ungulates or hoofed animals, which include deer, antelopes, cattle, pigs, and rhinos, form one of the largest groups of prey animals in Chitwan. These animals have limbs and feet designed to ensure speed and safety of movement, both essential elements for rapid flight when pursued by predators. Most ungulates have cloven hooves. These are adapted for continuous rough use and provide a good hold on uneven ground. On soft ground the two halves of the hoof spread, giving a better grip.

Chital (*Axis axis*) are the most common deer in the Park. Although they are usually seen feeding in the riverine forest during morning and late afternoon, they are also crop raiders, with large herds of them coming out to adjacent fields at night. Distinctively white-spotted, the graceful chital is considered one of the most beautiful of all deer. Mature males grow to about a metre at the shoulder and have long, three-tined antlers. The main rutting season seems to be between March and June, and although most young are born in winter, a few fawns are seen in all seasons. Only one fawn is born after a gestation period of about 7 months, with females going into oestrus again very soon after.

The **hog deer** (*Axis porcinus*), a close relative of the chital, with which it interbreeds, is named because of its thickset appearance and peculiar gait when running. This wary animal is not as common as the chital and is only seen in small groups in grasslands. Standing about 65 cm at the shoulder, the hog deer has a red-brown coat which is lightly spotted, but nowhere near as conspicuously as that of the chital. The stags have three-tined antlers, mounted on bony pedicles.

The **barking deer** or **muntjac** (*Muntiacus muntjak*) is smaller still at only 50–60 cm. Its loud, sharp call, much like the bark of a dog, is often heard in the early morning or evening. These reddish-brown deer usually move alone or in pairs, keeping within the forests. Their short antlers, growing backwards from long, hairy pedicles, are set at too acute an angle to be of much use to the stags when fighting during the rutting season. Instead, long sharp canine teeth, which project a little below the lips, are used. One white-spotted fawn is born after a 6-month gestation period. The spots fade when the fawn is about 6 months old.

The **sambar** (*Cervus unicolor*), an impressive animal, is the largest deer in Chitwan. Standing almost 1.5 m at the shoulder, and weighing up to 320 kg, mature stags carry large antlers and grow a thick ruff of hair around their necks. When in groups, sambar utter a loud, harsh bellow if alarmed, to warn the rest of the herd. Single animals usually stand still or slip quietly away almost unnoticed. During the peak of the rutting season in winter, stags combat one another for mates and territory. Females produce one fawn about 8 months later.

Serow and four-horned antelope also inhabit Chitwan but are rarely seen as they prefer the remote, forested ridges of the hills. The **serow** (*Capricornis sumatraensis*) has a coarse, hairy coat that varies from dark to mid-brown along the back and neck, with lighter underparts and legs. A disproportionately large head and long legs contribute to a rather ungainly appearance which belies the serow's sure-footedness. Gestation lasts 7 months, with usually only one kid born at a time.

The **four-horned antelope** (*Tetraceros quadricornis*) was only recently discovered in Chitwan, in the lower eastern foothills. Males have four horns, the back pair curving steeply upward and inward, the front pair very short and vertical. Females are hornless. These slender-legged antelopes live either singly or in pairs. When mating during the summer months, the males become very aggressive. Usually one young is produced after a 6-month gestation period.

Wild boar (*Sus scrofa*) are another common ungulate in Chitwan. Although occasionally seen alone, they usually congregate in groups. Almost black, and covered with coarse hair which rises in a dorsal mane of black bristles, adults measure about 75 cm at the shoulder and can weigh up to 160 kg. In contrast, the piglets are a light brown with dark stripes. They are profuse breeders, so it is not unusual to come across litters of up to six piglets, which are born in a nest of grass and other vegetation built by the sow before their birth in March–April.

The largest deer in the Park, the chital (above) and sambur (above right), are a tiger's main prey species.

At a lower level in the food chain, the hog deer (below), a smaller relative of the chital, and the tiny barking deer (right) are preyed on by leopards.

Adults have razor-sharp tusks and are formidable opponents of tigers and leopards, their natural predators and enemies. They can move with lightning speed and will also attack men or other animals much larger than themselves if threatened. Being omnivorous, wild boar will eat snakes, insects and carrion and dig for roots and tubers. They frequently raid village crops and are understandably the target of villagers' wrath.

Almost as large as the rhino, but more majestic looking, the **gaur** (*Bos gaurus*) is the largest of all wild cattle and is closely related to the domestic variety. Old bulls, their massive black bodies supported by slim, white-stockinged legs, can stand up to 1.8 m at the shoulder and weigh up to 1000 kg. A large dorsal ridge, chin and chest dewlaps, and heavy, black-tipped horns curving forward and upward from a whitish forehead, all enhance the impression of power. Cows are smaller and dark brown; the calves are born a golden-yellow. Most calves are born during spring, in secluded places away from the rest of the herd, and are able to walk within 20 minutes.

In spite of its powerful appearance, the gaur is a shy animal with a keen sense of smell but poor eyesight and hearing. Small herds inhabit the sal (*Shorea robusta*) forests of the Siwaliks most of the year, only descending to the plains during the hot dry season. They are attracted by water, which by then is scarce in the hills.

A fully grown gaur bull is an impressive animal.

Primates

Swinging and leaping from tree to tree with seemingly reckless abandon, a troupe of **common langurs** (*Presbytis entellus*) is a delight to watch. These handsome grey monkeys, their black faces ruffed with very pale fur, have long tails which they use for balance during their arboreal pursuits, practised while feeding on fruits, flower buds, leaves and other vegetable matter. Activity begins early in the day, usually at first light. After a few hours of rest in the middle of the day, foraging continues during the afternoon. By sundown, after a noisy spell, the langurs have usually retired for the night, to sleep in the outer branches of tall trees where they are safe from predators such as leopards.

Considered sacred because of their association with the monkey god Hanuman, langurs are not harmed by Hindus. They are adaptable animals and are able to live successfully in cold conifer forests up to 3660 m as well as the jungles of the Terai. Troupes are of two kinds: either all male, or else a harem with one or occasionally the largest male dominating the group. The young, born after about 6 months' gestation, cling with amazing tenacity to their mothers' bellies for the first few months of life. Although big enough to move around by themselves, they remain with their mothers until about a year old.

The **rhesus monkey** (*Macaca mulatta*) is much smaller than the langur, and, with its rather scruffy, yellow-brown fur and short tail, is nowhere near as handsome. It is one of the common monkeys in Asia and is often seen around temples in the Kathmandu Valley. Here it is very bold, but in the Park it is shy and avoids contact with humans. Rhesus monkeys are also considered sacred by Hindus.

In contrast to the arboreal langur, rhesus monkeys live more on the ground, where they search for vegetable matter and insects, only taking to the trees to avoid predators and to rest. They are fast eaters, stuffing their enlarged cheek pouches with half-eaten food and munching it later in a more relaxed fashion when in a secure place.

During oestrus, the normally pink-coloured faces of the females become reddish, and external areas of their genitals swell and become bright red. Mating usually takes place during the winter months and babies are born in late spring.

Rodents

Rodents are numerous and inhabit all environments of the Park, providing food for many carnivores. Bright brown with white underparts, and about the size of a house mouse, the **longtailed tree mouse** (*Vandeleuria oleracea*) lives an arboreal life. Its hands and feet are adapted to climbing branches, and even the young are born in nests built in trees.

Indian mole rats (*Bandicota bengalensis*) are the bane of local farmers because of their mole-like burrowing in fields and their habit of

A troupe of langurs can be noisy as it moves through the tree tops.

hoarding large quantities of corn under the ground. After harvesting a crop, farmers dig around the mole rats' nests to recover stolen grain. In appearance and size, mole rats are similar to the common rat but they have paler underparts. Being prolific breeders, they are very common.

Less common, the **great bandicoot** (*Bandicota indica*) lives in the grasslands and forests. This much larger rodent, with a body measuring up to 30 cm and weighing over 1 kg, is eaten with relish by some Terai people. It has a thick black tail and is usually dark grey and brown on the upper body and paler underneath.

Slightly smaller, the **bay bamboo rat** (*Canomys badius*) is chestnut coloured and has a very short tail. It has large claws for burrowing, and well developed incisors for gnawing at roots and other vegetation. Soft, dense fur completely covers its small ears.

Like many of its relatives, the **Indian porcupine** (*Hystrix indica*) is mainly nocturnal and is therefore not often seen. Adults can grow to 90 cm and weigh over 18 kg. Long sharp bristles and a profuse armoury of spines and quills on its back and tail make this large rodent no easy prey. To warn potential predators, the white, open-ended tail quills produce a rattling sound when shaken. Those on the back are black, brown and white striped. They are extremely sharp and easily removed as they are a form of modified hair. The belief that porcupines can shoot quills backwards is not correct but has probably arisen because of the animal's ability to move quickly backwards, ramming its quills into an adversary. Large predators such as tigers and leopards are known to have died from infections caused by porcupine quills embedded in their flesh.

A resident of sal forest and grasslands, the porcupine lives in burrows which it usually excavates near streams and ravines. The burrow entrance is often littered with gnawed bones and antlers scavenged from tiger and leopard kills. These furnish the porcupine with calcium and minerals for quill growth. The rest of its diet is made up of vegetable matter.

Chitwan has several species of squirrels. Largest is the **giant flying squirrel** (*Petaurista petaurista*), with adults measuring almost a metre from nose to tail-tip. A stretchy membrane between its limbs acts like a parachute when they are spread out, enabling the animal to make long gliding leaps of over 75 m. This handsome creature has a dark reddish-brown back, light-coloured belly, and a long, thick bushy tail. It sleeps through the day, in nests or holes in tree trunks, with its body rolled up and head bent forward; at night it leaps from tree to tree in search of fruits, nuts, bark and new shoots.

The **parti-coloured flying squirrel** (*Hylopetes alboniger*) is much smaller, with dark brownish-grey fur mixed with black on its back, and white underparts. Like the giant flying squirrel, it prefers hill forests, where it builds nests of grass in the trees.

Another forest dweller and nest builder, the **hoary-bellied Himalayan squirrel** (*Callosciurus pygerythrus*), measures only 40 cm from nose to tail-tip. This dark, rufous-brown squirrel with a greyish or pale rufous belly has a surprisingly loud call.

Two species of palm squirrel are very common and often seen because of their diurnal habits. Both feed on seeds, fruits, and other vegetation.

Three-striped palm squirrel.

The **five-striped palm squirrel** (*Funambulus pennanti*) prefers to be near human habitation. It has five pale stripes running the length of its brownish-grey body and measures up to 30 cm from nose to tail-tip. The **three-striped palm squirrel** (*Funambulus palmarum*) is a forest dweller. It has three yellowish stripes and makes bird-like, chirruping calls. Nests of large, rough grasses or fibres are made in tree branches.

Hares and rabbits are among the rodents known best to mankind. True rabbits, which give birth to naked and blind young, are not found in Nepal but hares are. One species, the **Indian hare** (*Lepus nigricollis ruficaudatus*), lives in the grasslands of Chitwan. It has a light reddish-brown coat with lighter underparts , characteristic long ears and legs, and can weigh up to 2.5 kg with a body length of 50 cm. Like other hares, its young, born with fur and open eyes, are capable of moving with their parent almost immediately after birth.

The extremely rare **hispid hare** (*Caprolagus hispidus*) is suspected to be in Chitwan. It was recently found in Royal Suklaphanta Wildlife Reserve in west Nepal, but very few have ever been caught since the species was first discovered by Sir Brian Hodgson in 1848. Very little is known about the hispid hare because of its shy, secretive nature. It is distinguished from the Indian hare by its short ears and much darker, almost blackish-brown fur with numerous bristly hairs through it. A recent study indicates that the hispid hare is more akin to rabbits than to hares.

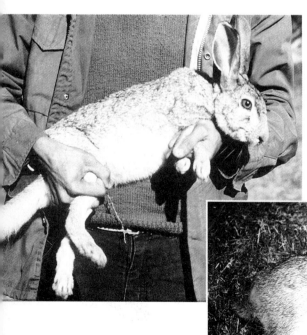

The rufous-tailed hare (left) is common in the Park's grasslands, but the rare hispid hare has yet to be recorded there. The one shown below was photographed in west Nepal after being trodden on by an elephant.

Bats

Bats, the true flying mammals of the animal kingdom, are common in the Terai. They are frequently seen in the Park at dusk, flitting silently between trees like fleeting, ghostly shadows. By day they hang from trees, motionless and upside-down, with wings folded. Bats are classified in two groups according to their diet: the *Megachiroptera* — the larger fruit-eating bats or flying foxes — and the *Microchiroptera*, which are small and insectivorous.

The *Megachiroptera* are represented by three species. The **large fruit bat** (*Pteropus giganticus*) is the most visible and is the species often seen in tall trees in Kathmandu and Bhaktapur. The **short-nosed fruit bat** (*Cynopterus sphinx*) and **Leschenault's fruit bat** (*Rousettus leschenaulti*) are also common. All feed on flowers and fruits, preferably mangoes, and are often considered pests.

The insectivorous *Microchiroptera* are represented by at least three species. The **great eastern horseshoe bat** (*Rhinolophus luctus*) has almost black, woolly-looking fur, and a long protruding nose leaf overlapping its mouth. The **Coromandel** or **Indian pipistrelle** (*Pipistrellus coromandra*), a much smaller species, is usually dark brown with paler underparts. Well camouflaged by their orange bodies and black-and-orange wings, **painted bats** (*Kerivoula picta*) are not often seen when they roost in trees among dead leaves.

Many other species may occur in the Park, but without further studies these strange mammals will remain unknown entities.

Fruit bats decorate a tree by day, waiting for nightfall when they will fly out to feed.

Pangolins

Pangolins or **scaly anteaters** (*Manis pentadactyla*) are undoubtedly the strangest mammals found in Chitwan. With their bodies almost covered by tile-shaped, overlapping yellowish-brown scales, a form of modified hair, they look more like reptiles than mammals. Their bellies and the insides of their legs are soft though, and covered with small, sparse hairs. The pangolin's body is perfectly adapted to a diet of termites and ants. With its long, forked sticky tongue darting rapidly in and out, a pangolin can quickly devour the contents of an ant or termite nest after opening it with its strong, curved claws. The nostrils are closed while feeding and thick eyelids give protection against stings and bites. Pangolins have no teeth. Insects are ground up inside the stomach by a set of pyloric teeth and stones which are also swallowed.

Balancing with their tails, pangolins often stand on their hindquarters while sniffing out food. They are even capable of running on their hind feet. At night, much of their time is spent in trees, clinging to branches with their prehensile tails. During the heat of the day they retreat to the coolness of chambers lying 3–4 m deep in the ground.

A master of self-defence, when threatened the pangolin will roll into a tight ball to protect its soft underparts, exhibiting extraordinary strength against attempts to unroll it. Unfortunately these inoffensive creatures are hunted because many parts of their bodies are considered to have medicinal properties. In the past they were kept as pets and sold in the bazaars of Kathmandu. Being slow breeders with a short lifespan, they are now very rare.

Adult pangolins can grow to a metre in length. At birth they weigh about 500 g and measure 45 cm, and their scales are soft and flexible. Babies are unable to walk and are carried on their mothers' backs and tails. If danger threatens, they cling underneath, protected by a pouch formed when the mother folds her tail.

Exceptions to the Rule

There are always exceptions to every rule, and a few animals are neither predator nor prey. Chitwan's two largest herbivores, the rhinoceros and elephant, and the omnivorous sloth bear are not normally attacked by any predator because of their size and strength. As with tigers, their greatest enemy is Man.

Rhinos

Massive, stumpy-legged and prehistoric in appearance, the **greater Asian one-horned rhinoceros** (*Rhinoceros unicornis*) is the largest ungulate in Chitwan. Thanks to conservation efforts, it can be frequently sighted. Large males average almost 2 m at the shoulder and weigh up to 2

(Below) Fighting between male rhinos is frequent and vicious, with severe wounds inflicted by sharp, tusk-like teeth on the lower jaw (above).

(Opposite) A tranquillised rhino is loaded into a crate for translocation to Royal Bardia National Park in west Nepal.

tonnes. In spite of their clumsy appearance, rhinos are extremely agile and capable of making high-speed turns when charging. Usually such charges are of a threatening nature and are not repeated unless the rhino is seriously provoked. Females with calves are very protective, however, and will charge instinctively. Approaching rhinos on foot is extremely dangerous and a few visitors and locals are gored every year.

The rhino's thick, leathery hide is practically hairless and studded with round, warty tubercles. Several deep folds around the body give an armour-plated appearance. The single horn, a mass of cemented, fibrous hair, is not attached to the skull but is supported by enlarged nasal bones. Growth of the horn continues throughout the rhino's life and if broken off, it can regrow. Although the largest recorded length for a horn is 60 cm, most average around 20 cm. The purpose of a rhino's horn is not known. An elongated and pointed upper lip overhangs a pair of tusk-like teeth which protrude from the lower jaw. These can inflict deep cuts. Fighting between males is frequent, and injured animals have been known to die from infected wounds.

In Nepal and the Far East many parts of the rhino's body are thought to hold medicinal properties. Powdered horn is considered to be exceptionally good, although its powers have yet to be proven scientifically. It is not generally used as an aphrodisiac except in a few parts of India. The meat is supposed to induce vigour, and the urine is used as a remedy against asthma, stomachache and tuberculosis.

Male rhinos urinate backwards, often spraying urine a considerable distance. They usually defecate in the same place, producing dung piles at selected sites. Fresh dung appears to be a stimulus to defecate, and calves will defecate immediately after their mothers. After inspecting a latrine site, a rhino will back up to it and add to the pile, an act which seems to be an important means of communication between individuals.

Rhinos' eyesight is very poor and they can hardly see further than 100 m. Poor sight is compensated, however, by good olfactory and auditory powers.

The lifespan of a rhino is 60 to 70 years and sexual maturity is reached around 10 years of age. Breeding occurs throughout the year and mating takes place when both male and female come on heat. Mating usually takes place after a courtship of 3 or 4 days. Only one calf is born after a gestation period of 18–19 months. At birth the calf is pink, and it is able to follow its mother immediately. Mother and calf usually stay together for at least 3 years before separating, after which the cow comes on heat again.

Like the tigers, the rhinos of Chitwan have been the subject of intensive study since 1973. Rhinos have also been immobilised and fitted with radio collars, a technique which makes it easier to take measurements and to track their movements.

Until recently, Chitwan was the only place in Nepal where rhinos remained. The possibility that an epidemic could wipe out the whole population remained a constant threat, despite the fact that their numbers have increased from less than 100 in 1967 to more than 350 at present. As insurance against this happening, 13 rhinos were recently relocated to Royal Bardia National Park, 300 km away in the western Terai. Studies and monitoring programmes indicate that the translocated rhinos have settled into their new habitat. Early in 1988 one female produced a calf, but it will be some time before the real success or failure of this venture is known. If the results are promising, more rhinos may be relocated.

Elephants

The **Asian elephant** (*Elephas maximus*) is Chitwan's largest animal, with fully grown adults weighing up to 6 tonnes. Once common in the Terai, wild elephants are now a rare sight, with only a few small groups remaining in southern border areas of Nepal. Unlike the seemingly docile, obedient elephants used to transport tourists, the wild animal can be extremely dangerous when confronted on its own territory. Even trained elephants have occasionally killed their trainers and should be approached cautiously.

An elephant consumes 250–350 kg of forage each day. Vegetable matter provides more fibre than protein and an adult needs to forage for most of the day to get enough nutrients. Browsing at a height of about 5 m, a herd of elephants will rip branches and leaves from trees, and even uproot them occasionally. This creates gaps in the forest canopy and alters the ecosystem. Grasses are also uprooted and eaten once the soil has been knocked off the roots by the elephant's agile trunk.

Elephants do not have canine teeth and their incisors are modified into tusks. To grind up fibrous vegetation they have four ridged molar teeth which are replaced as they wear out. During its life an elephant goes through six sets of teeth, each new set being larger and lasting longer than the previous one. The final teeth appear when the elephant is about 60 years of age and last the rest of the animal's life.

Herds usually consist of family groups of mainly females and their offspring, with one elderly cow as the matriarch. Males tend to live on their own, pushed out of the herd when they attain sexual maturity between 10 and 15 years of age. They occasionally gather in small groups in the vicinity of the females, with one large bull as the leader. Only when in heat do males associate with females and this may be several times a year. Bulls will fight savage duels over mating rights and some end in death.

Gestation takes about 22 months. While giving birth the cow assumes a squatting position and is surrounded by other cows of the same herd. To dry the new calf, cows blow dust over it. Standing about a metre high and weighing about 90 kg at birth, a baby elephant is covered with yellow and brown hair. When suckling from its mother's two teats, which hang between her forelegs, the calf drinks from the side of its mouth. A calf depends on its mother's milk for almost 4 years and if she dies it will be nursed by another lactating cow.

Elephants need to drink up to 205 litres of water a day. During dry times they will dig holes at moist places in dry riverbeds to get at underground water, opening up watering-holes which other animals can also use. Because they are so massive, with a low ratio of surface to body mass, it is difficult for elephants to dissipate their body heat through surface radiation. For this reason they like to bathe or spray themselves. When water is not available they will suck saliva from their mouths and squirt it over their bodies. After bathing, elephants often wallow in dust or mud which dries to a light-coloured coating which is insect-proof and less heat absorbent. Their large, leathery ears have numerous blood vessels on the back surface. This helps to regulate body temperature through surface radiation. As the animal ages its ears lose some of their normal grey pigmentation, turning pinkish and spotted along the top edge, which folds forward.

Because of their tremendous weight, elephants must rest standing up or their internal organs would be damaged. Thick, pillar-like legs with flat-surfaced joints, and large, round, thickly padded feet with heavy toenails give support but do not afford much flexibility in body movement. To compensate, the trunk has evolved as a powerful and

Elephants love a dust bath.

sensitive organ used in drinking, procuring food, spraying water, vocalisation and, most importantly, for smelling. Coordinating the movement of its trunk is a skill which a baby elephant learns instinctively.

Sloth bears

Broken termite mounds and diggings in the forest are trademarks of the **sloth bear** (*Melursus ursinus*), being the signs of quests for termites and ants, its staple food. A mobile snout aids the search and long, powerful, non-retractile claws easily rip open termite mounds. By licking and sucking the termites out with its long extensile tongue, the sloth bear quickly empties the mound. Sloth bears also climb trees to get fruit, flowers and honey, and will eat insects or even the remains of tiger kills.

Poor eyesight and hearing make this animal an unpredictable creature when cornered or surprised. In spite of its name, the sloth bear can move very fast, inflicting dreadful wounds with its claws. It is therefore rated as the most dangerous animal in Chitwan. Although cubs can be preyed upon by tigers and leopards, adults are left alone because of their size and strength. Males stand at just under 2 m and weigh up to 135 kg. Unlike the Himalayan black bear (*Selenarctos thibetanus*), the sloth bear does not hibernate in winter. The cubs are born at this time, after 6 months' gestation, and females are often seen in spring with one or two lying crosswise on their backs.

An unpredictable temper, speed and long, curved claws combine to make the sloth bear one of the most dangerous animals in Chitwan.

Inhabitants of the Aquatic Environment

Otters
Master of the river, where it preys on fish, the **smooth Indian otter** (*Lutra perspicillata*) also hunts on land for frogs, insects and ground birds. Webbed feet, a sleek body and a flattened muscular tail covered with dark brown, waterproof fur, allow this mustelid to move swiftly in pursuit of aquatic prey. Ears and nostrils which can be closed when under water are other adaptations to an aquatic lifestyle. Weighing about 10 kg, otters can measure up to 1.2 m in length, including their tails.

Breeding is reported to take place between November and February. Gestation is about 2 months and the young are believed to stay with the mother for 10–12 months. During the day otters hide in holes in the root systems of riverside trees, or else in burrows in sandy banks where there is thick vegetation.

Each otter has a territory covering about 8–10 km of river, marked out with spraints (faecal droppings). The spraints are deposited either singly, on prominent rocks or logs, or on sand mounds scraped up to mark territory, or else in groups on dry sand and shingle banks. Being secretive and nocturnal, little else is known about these animals, which are now becoming rare in Nepal.

Dolphins
One of the most endangered of all Chitwan's mammals is the freshwater **Gangetic dolphin** (*Platanista gangetica*). Typically dolphin-like in appearance, these mammals inhabit the upper reaches of the rivers of India and Nepal for most of the year. Although they migrate to tidal waters during the monsoon, they never enter the sea. Unfortunately the dolphins which migrate down the Narayani River are unable to return because the irrigation dam at Tribenighat does not have fish ladders by which they can ascend. The dam also causes silting of the river, reducing its depth and changing the deepwater environment which dolphins like.

Gangetic dolphins are usually solitary but at times associate in small groups. They betray their presence when they rise to the surface to breathe, exhaling air from a narrow, slit-like blowhole on the top of the head. Their small eyes have poor vision, but this is compensated by their sensitive snout, which probes for fish, shrimps and other organisms in the river-bottom mud. Adults are normally about 2 m long, females being larger than males. They become sexually mature in 1 year. Only one young, weighing around 7 kg and measuring about 45 cm is born after a gestation period of 240-270 days. Being mammals, the young are suckled with milk by their mothers.

These fascinating, docile creatures were once seen regularly near the confluence of the Narayani and Rapti rivers, but sightings are now rare. Local people do not kill them but will use the blubber and meat if they find a dead one. The meat is considered very tasty and the oil is believed to have medicinal qualities.

Crocodiles

Lying motionless, almost completely submerged and invisible except for the bulbous tip of its snout and periscopic eyes, a **gharial crocodile** (*Gavialis gangeticus*) surveys the river scenery. If no danger threatens, it draws itself slowly up on to the sandy riverbank to bask in the sun. At the slightest alarm the reptile will retreat quickly to the safety of the river.

It is not only physical danger but extinction which threatens this extremely rare species. Distribution of the gharial is limited to a few isolated places in the headwaters of the Brahmaputra and Ganges river systems, which in Nepal includes the Narayani, Babai and Karnali rivers. Because of loss and disturbance of habitat, human interference and competition for food by fishermen, Chitwan gharials were estimated to number fewer than 50 in 1977.

Overfishing and water pollution are possibly limiting factors in the gharial's ability to breed. Increased siltation above the dam at Tribenighat raises the water level during floods, adversely affecting breeding sites on sandbanks. Many of these nesting sites were once safe from monsoon floods but are now inundated when the river rises. Human populations living along the riverbanks also force the gharial to use less than ideal sites for nests. Eggs are stolen by otters, jackals, wild boar and lizards, and also by humans who consider them to have medicinal properties. The chances of survival for hatchlings in the wild are extremely poor and less than 2 per cent live to become adults.

It was obvious that drastic steps would have to be taken to save the species from extinction. In 1978 an artificial hatching and rearing centre was established at Kasara, the Park Headquarters. Gharial eggs were collected by local fishermen, who knew where nests were located. At first the eggs were reburied in sandbanks but it has since proved more successful to hatch them in artificial nests. In captive conditions the hatching success rate is 60–70 per cent. The baby gharials are reared in tanks at Kasara for 2 to 3 years. Once they reach a length of about 1.5 m they are released into the wild. A total of 272 gharials have been released to date: 155 in the Narayani River, 35 in the Kali Gandaki, and 82 in the Kosi.

With its streamlined body and long, powerful tail, the gharial is well adapted to living in rivers. It lives entirely on fish, which are snapped up with jerking, sideways movements of the long snout. Although posing no threat to humans, gharials are poached for their olive-green

The rare, slender-snouted gharial is a river dweller, which feeds only on fish. To save the gharial from extinction, its eggs are collected and the young are raised in captivity.

Lured close by a log-like pose, unwary animals are snatched by the marsh mugger's powerful jaws, then drowned and torn to pieces.

skin and killed by fishermen when they become entangled in nets. Local people also consider the eggs, penis and bulbous protuberance on the gharial's snout to have aphrodisiac properties.

Mating takes place in winter. Later, in March to early April, the females dig holes about 50 cm deep in which the eggs are laid in two or three layers and covered with sand. A maximum of 96 eggs has been recorded in the Park. Depending on the temperature of the nest, the optimum being 31° C, the eggs hatch in July after 70–90 days of incubation. Under natural conditions the female usually remains in the vicinity of the nest to protect the eggs against predators. Newly hatched gharial young measure about 30 cm and have small yolk sacs to nourish them for a few days. They usually grow to about 5 m long, although specimens measuring nearly 7 m have been recorded.

Unlike the river-dwelling gharial, the smaller **marsh mugger** (*Crocodylus palustris*) prefers swamps and oxbow lakes, although it is seen occasionally in rivers. A short, blunt snout and cruel, wavy-looking mouth distinguish this crocodile from the slender-snouted gharial. The mugger also lies motionless, basking for hours on banks in winter. To move quickly enough to capture prey, it must raise the temperature of its cold-blooded body. During the hot summer months muggers do not bask but lie in the water with their mouths open to cool off.

A motionless pose enables the omnivorous mugger to blend with the environment. Any unwary animal which wanders within range is seized with surprising speed and agility and then dragged into the water and drowned. Internal nostrils opening deep in the throat can be closed with valves, enabling the mugger to hold struggling prey submerged without inhaling water itself. The prey, which can be as large as deer, is then torn apart and swallowed in chunks. Other food is mainly fish and small aquatic creatures, and muggers also scavenge.

The mugger also lays its eggs late in the dry season in a hole scooped in a bank. Up to 40 eggs are laid and the female stays nearby to guard them from potential predators until the young hatch in July. Like gharials, the ready-to-hatch young give "hatching" calls which stimulate the mother to excavate the nest and later lead them to water. The mortality rate of hatchlings is high, many being eaten by storks, jackals, otters and monitor lizards before they are a month old.

Even though it is not quite as threatened as the gharial, the marsh mugger is nevertheless an endangered species because of human interference and destruction of its habitat.

Turtles and tortoises
The rivers and lakes of Chitwan provide ideal habitat for at least four species of turtle. Largest is the **freshwater narrow-headed soft-shell turtle** (*Chitra indica*) which has a carapace (upper shell) up to 80 cm long.

Olive to grey in colour, with black and yellow streaks, the disk-shaped carapace is flexible and covered with skin instead of hard scutes, while the plastron or lower shell is white. As the name also suggests, this turtle has a long, narrow head ending in a snout and short proboscis. Fish, molluscs and other animals form its diet. Nesting is thought to take place during the monsoon, with about 100 eggs being laid.

Similar but smaller, the **Indian soft-shell turtle** (*Trionyx gangeticus*) has black oblique streaks on a greenish head. It also has a long neck and a proboscis on its snout. Usually up to 35 eggs are laid during the monsoon or shortly afterwards.

Both the two other aquatic turtles belong to the genus *Kachuga*. They have characteristic hard shells covered with plates of material similar to human fingernails. They feed on plant and animal matter. The **three-striped roofed turtle** (*Kachuga dhongoka*) has an olive to brown carapace with three black stripes, and a yellowish plastron. A yellowish line runs along its head from the tip of its snout. Nests containing 30–35 eggs are dug in riverbanks during the dry season.

The **red-crowned roofed turtle** (*Kachuga kachuga*) has an olive to brown body and a carapace with no markings. During the breeding season the head develops a bright red patch on the top and blue areas on the sides; the neck has red and yellow stripes. Females of both species measure about 50 cm; the males are just over half this size.

Two other species found in Chitwan are primarily terrestrial. The **East Asian tortoise** (*Indotestudo engata*) lives in the sal forests. It has elephant-like rear legs, a yellowish head and a helmet-like carapace with black blotches. The **tricarinate hill turtle** (*Melanochelys tricarinata*) has a black carapace and two broad, reddish-brown stripes on each side of its head. It lays its three to six eggs in piles of rhino dung and is often seen during the monsoon in wet depressions in the grasslands.

Fish

Over 70 species of fish live in the waters of the Narayani, Rapti and Reu rivers and their tributaries, offering a variety of food for water-dwelling animals. Otters seem to prefer *Mystus* species, *Puntius* species and **bitti** (*Danio devario*). The bitti is a small fish found in shallow inlets and small tributaries. It has a deep cylindrical body, greenish above and silvery below, with a short, dark stripe starting from the tail.

Puntius, known locally as **sidra**, are very small, silvery fish with two dark spots, one near the tail and the other near the gills. Shoals of tiny sidra swimming in shallow water at river edges and in inlets and small tributaries are easy prey for wading birds. They are also common in ponds where they are eaten by herons, kingfishers and crocodiles. *Mystus*, predatory catfish known locally as **tengna** or **tengri**, have elongated bodies, small eyes and four pairs of long barbels that stream backwards like cat's whiskers.

Goranhi (*Chagunius chagunia*), **mahseer** (*Tor tor*), **rotar** (*Tor putitora*) and several species of *Labeo* and *Barilius* are other fish common in shallow water near riverbanks. The goranhi, a pink-tinged silvery fish with tile-like scales, is important to local people for food as it can grow to 45 cm long. *Labeo* have long bodies with round bellies and fleshy lips and snouts. The trout-like *Barilius* are medium-sized fish with longish bodies and small scales.

Because they grow to a large size, mahseer and rotar are popular game and food fish. The rotar has an olive-green back, pinkish sides and a silvery belly. The mahseer has similar colouring but with an overall golden tinge instead of pink, and reddish-yellow lower fins.

Two other interesting fish which live under stones in fast-flowing water are *Botia* species. *B. lohachata* has a pointed mouse-like head with six to eight pairs of barbels. Its yellow body has distinct "Y"-shaped dark bands and the fins have black stripes. *B. almorhae* is similar, with a yellowish body marked with a grey pattern.

Lizards and Snakes

Lizards
Visitors need not search hard to find lizards in Chitwan. The common **garden lizard** (*Calotes versicolor*) prefers open areas and is often seen on posts or in shrubbery around villages, or in open sunny forest. Being mainly arboreal and agile, with a compressed body, long tail and hind legs, the garden lizard easily avoids capture. Its scaly, light-brown skin, marked with a few narrow dark bars on the tail and a light side stripe, provides excellent camouflage. A row of spiny projections along the back makes this lizard appear fiercer than it really is. During the breeding season males become bright reddish-orange on the front half of their bodies.

While the garden lizard is a "sit-and-wait" hunter, moving only when an insect is sighted, three other diurnal lizards search actively for food. These are all skinks — smooth, shiny lizards usually found on the ground searching for prey under leaf litter and logs. The largest of these skinks, *Mabuya dissimilis*, is usually seen in grasslands. Growing to about 10 cm, this species is olive-brown with paired white spots on its back and a pair of stripes and numerous white spots on each side.

Smaller, and more heavy-bodied, with short legs, *Mabuya macularia* prefers forest edges and is sometimes seen on logs in patches of sunlight. Adults are brown with a broad, dark stripe along the back; juveniles have numerous white spots on the sides of the neck and fore body.

Scincella sikkimensis is the smallest skink, measuring only 3–3.5 cm. It spends most of its life beneath logs and litter on the forest floor.

The garden lizard (above) waits for insect prey to come close whereas the yellow monitor (left) hunts birds and small animals in trees. Monitors can grow to a metre in length.

Geckos — nocturnal lizards with large, unlidded eyes — are represented by two species. The **yellow-bellied house gecko** (*Hemidactylus flaviviridis*), the larger and rarer of the two, is distinguished by its yellowish belly and the uniform granular scales on its back. **Brook's gecko** (*Hemidactylus brookii*) has a few larger tubercles with the granular scales, and a white underside. The yellow-bellied gecko is found only in houses but Brook's gecko is also found in forests, hiding under logs or leaf litter in tree buttresses. Both species mate and lay eggs in the late dry season and early monsoon.

Denizens of the forests and predators of snakes, lizards, birds and small mammals, the short-legged monitors are the largest lizards. The **yellow monitor** (*Varanus flavescens*) is common in the Park and is often seen climbing trees. It is yellowish-brown in colour. The much larger but rarer **Indian monitor** (*Varanus bengalensis*) has an olive-brown skin and hunts for its prey in grasslands and on the forest floor. Both have extremely sharp teeth which can inflict nasty wounds.

Snakes

Much feared but rarely seen by Park visitors are a variety of snakes. Most are shy of humans and many hibernate during winter. The colourfully patterned **Indian python** (*Python molurus*) is the largest. Although the specimens recorded in Chitwan are smaller, lengths of up to 5.85 m have been recorded elsewhere. Inhabitants of sal and riverine forest, pythons catch prey by striking with their fangs, then squeezing

Colour is the only physical characteristic that the harmless tree snake (top left) and the venomous bamboo pit viper (top right) share. The striped keelback (right) and chequered keelback (above) both prey on small creatures whereas the python (below), a huge snake, will kill animals as large as deer.

Python swallowing a deer.

the victim with their coils until it suffocates. The dead prey is then swallowed whole as the python's jaws are connected by very elastic muscles and can separate widely. It may take several hours to ingest a large deer, after which a python can go without more food for weeks. Unlike most snakes, the female python coils herself around her eggs, not only to protect them but to keep them from becoming cold. The eggs are laid from March through to June and hatch during the monsoon.

At the opposite end of the scale is the tiny **blind snake** (*Rhamphotyphlops braminus*) which grows to less than 20 cm. This dark-brown or black, earthworm-like reptile has only vestigial eyes and a blunt nose. During the day the blind snake searches for termites and worms, burrowing into the ground with a spine on the tip of its tail. It lays from two to seven eggs in the late dry season.

Between these two extremes are dozens of other species, some venomous and others completely harmless. Most of the non-venomous measure between 0.5 and 2 m in length, and have a wide variety of colours and patterns. Some are egg-layers and others give birth to live young.

One of the more unusual is the **green tree** or **whip snake** (*Ahaetulla nasuta*). Measuring up to 2 m long, this slender, bright green creature lives in trees and is camouflaged by its colour and long slender snout. To complete the picture, the whip snake will often sway its body from side to side like a branch. Up to 23 young are born during the dry season.

As its name suggests, the harmless **rat snake** (*Ptyas mucosus*) is a rodent, frog and toad hunter. It has an overall brown colour and usually grows to about 2 m. Females lay 6-14 eggs during the dry season and coil around them until they hatch.

The **Indian gamma** or **catsnake** (*Boiga trigonata*), named because of its catlike eyes with vertical pupils, is not quite as harmless. Although only about a metre long, this yellowish-grey to brown snake with irregular white crossbars should be treated with caution as it is slightly venomous. A catsnake will coil and strike at the slightest provocation, inflating and deflating its body repeatedly and rapidly vibrating its tail in a very threatening way. Normally an arboreal lizard-eater, it will also prey on small birds. Rarely seen, the **tawny catsnake** (*B. ochracea*) also occurs in Chitwan. It is nocturnal but little else is known about it.

The non-poisonous common wolf snake is often confused with the venomous Indian krait. Both are dark snakes with light-coloured crossbars and white bellies, but each has distinguishing features. The **wolf snake** (*Lycodon aulicus*) is small and brown, and has a distinct head which is wider than the neck. It eats lizards and frogs and is often found under wood near human habitation. The common **Indian krait** (*Bungarus caeruleus*) is much larger and more black, with a shiny, bluish tinge. Unlike the wolf snake, it does not have a distinct head. During the day this krait hides in holes and crevices, only coming out at night to hunt other snakes and rodents. Kraits have the most potent venom of all the poisonous snakes in Chitwan, a neurotoxin which affects the central nervous system.

Five other non-poisonous snakes are the striped keelback, the trinket snake, the copperhead, the banded khukri, and the Indian bronzeback. The **striped keelback** (*Amphiesma stolata*), a small greenish-brown snake with two yellowish stripes, hunts frogs, toads and lizards and is very common. The **trinket snake** (*Elaphe helena*), a black, brown and white patterned species which grows to about a metre, and the larger **copperhead** (*E. radiata*) are found mainly in forests, where they hunt during the day for small mammals, lizards, frogs and other snakes.

The **banded khukri** (*Oligodon arnensis*) is often found near buildings, searching for the eggs of geckos and other reptiles. This very small black and brown snake gets its name from its upper rear teeth, which are shaped like a khukri knife. The **Indian bronzeback** (*Dendrelaphis tristis*), a common arboreal snake, hunts during the day for lizards, tree frogs and small birds. It has a purplish-brown back and yellow belly. When excited, the bronzeback will expand its neck, revealing a blue colour between the scales.

Slender and fast moving, the **condanarous sandsnake** (*Psammophis condanarous*) is found in grasslands and open forest. This dark striped, brown snake has enlarged rear fangs and should be treated as poisonous.

Although two species of cobra are found in the Park, they are not at all common. Largest of all poisonous snakes, the **king cobra** (*Ophiophagus hannah*) has been observed in the Siwalik Hills, but it is rare even here. Juveniles are vividly marked with alternating black and white crossbands, but these fade on adults. Although most king cobras average 3–4 m in length, they can grow to 5 m. During the late dry season the female builds a nest-mound of vegetation and lays 21–51 eggs in an inside chamber. She then coils herself on top or within a second, upper chamber and waits until the eggs hatch in the early monsoon. Because of the large quantities of venom injected, a bite by a king cobra is usually rapidly fatal from cardiac or respiratory arrest.

The **common cobra** (*Naja naja*) is seen more often around villages than in the Park. This shy snake will usually flee when disturbed, rather than attack. Its diet consists of small mammals, frogs, snakes, lizards and eggs. The common cobra's most distinctive feature is its ability to expand its neck to form a hood, marked on the back with yellow or orange. In the dry season 10 to 20 eggs are laid and both male and female guard the nest.

Three other poisonous snakes occurring in the Park are the bamboo pit viper, the banded krait and MacClelland's coral snake. The **bamboo pit viper** (*Trimeresurus albolabris*) inhabits sal and riverine forests. This completely green reptile is distinguished by its narrow neck, large triangular head and eyes with vertical pupils. Small and nocturnal, the bamboo pit viper locates prey in the dark with infra-red sensors located in deep pits on either side of the head. It is these pits which give pit vipers their name. They give birth to live young. Unlike that of other snakes, the venom of vipers affects red blood cells, causing haemorrhaging.

The venom of the **banded krait** (*Bungarus fasciatus*) is more potent than a cobra's, but it is a lethargic snake and is not common. It has black and yellow crossbars from head to tail-tip and a distinct ridge down its back. **MacClelland's coral snake** (*Callophis macclellandi*), a reddish species with black markings, is usually found in forests, where it preys on other snakes.

Two unusual snakes which have been recorded in Chitwan are the Indian egg-eating snake and the flying snake. The **egg-eating snake** (*Elachistodon westermanni*), as its name implies, eats only birds' eggs. It has only a few small teeth, but the lower spines of some anterior vertebrae penetrate the throat wall so that eggs are slit open as they pass to the stomach. The shells are regurgitated. This dark-coloured snake is very rare and little is known about it.

The colourful **flying snake** (*Crysopelia ornata*), named for its ability to glide from one tree branch to another, has a greenish-yellow body marked with black crossbars and red spots. Raised keels near the outside edges of the ventral plates assist in gliding and holding on to branches at the end of a flight. Lizards, especially geckos, snakes and small birds make up the flying snake's diet.

Two species of semi-aquatic snakes are found near watercourses where they hunt for fish, frogs and tadpoles. Both have strongly keeled scales, giving the body a rough appearance, and eyes located high on the head. The heavy-bodied **checkered keelback** (*Xenochropis piscator*) can be vicious when disturbed and will strike with great force. It often plays dead if attacked by a predator, twisting over and over as if dealt a lethal blow. The body is greenish-yellow with five rows of black spots. Up to 91 eggs are laid in the dry season, in a ground cavity near water. The **water snake** (*Homolopsis buccata*) has a green to purplish-coloured body and a white head with dark markings. From 9–21 offspring are born during the monsoon.

Frogs and Toads

Frogs and toads form an important part of the diet of snakes and large birds such as storks and herons. Some species are found near water; others are mainly terrestrial. Water is only necessary for their eggs, which are laid in great numbers in clumps and ropes of jelly, and for the

Toads are common in Chitwan and form an important link in the food chain.

Frogs are a favourite food of storks and herons. Small skittering frogs (left) rest at the edge of a pool until a disturbance sends them skating over the water's surface.

tadpoles. The eggs are frequently eaten by fish and thus the amphibians form an important link in the food chain.

Frogs are most evident during the monsoon, when males call to attract females. Breeding commences as soon as there is sufficient water for eggs and tadpoles. This also provides enough time for the tadpoles to metamorphose while insect prey is abundant. Both adults and juveniles must store sufficient body-energy reserves to be able to survive the dry season in an inactive state. During the early post-monsoon period the young frogs are seen hopping everywhere, but within a month their numbers are reduced by predators.

The warty-skinned toads are much more squat and shorter-legged than frogs. They have no teeth but have parotid glands which produce a viscous, milky fluid highly toxic to animal predators and humans.

Two species of toads are found in Chitwan. The larger and spinier of the two, *Bufo melanostictus*, measures 9–14 cm; the other, *B. stomaticus*, is usually between 4.5 and 7 cm in length. Both have small, spiny warts but in the former they are more numerous, larger and darker. *B. melanostictus* is common near agricultural areas while *B. stomaticus* prefers forest margins. Both breed in shallow ponds at the beginning of the monsoon, the only time they are found near water. The rest of the year is spent in dry areas, hiding beneath leaf litter during the day and foraging at night.

Hiding in trees and shrubbery is the attractive **tree frog** (*Polypedates maculatus*). Enlarged digital pads on its hands and feet enable the tree frog to climb vertical surfaces or to traverse narrow branches. This dark-spotted, greyish-brown species has a chocolate-brown eye-stripe extending from the tip of its snout to the sides of its body, and sports bright yellow spots on the groin and undersides of the thighs.

True frogs, belonging to the genus *Rana*, are represented in Chitwan by possibly as many as eight species but they are difficult to identify. The most obvious one is the olive to greyish-green **skittering frog** (*Rana cyanophlyctis*) which rests at the water's edge until a disturbance sends it skimming across the surface of the water.

Other frogs, such as *R. crassa* and *R. tigerina*, are more terrestrial and inhabit grasslands and forest margins. The two species are similar in appearance, with greenish-tan backs overlaid with dark coppery-brown spots, and thin cream stripes along the back and sides.

The **Indian cricket frogs** are also found in grassland, riverine and sal forests. Distinguished only by their breeding calls, cricket frogs are generally all dark brown to brownish-olive, with darker blotches on the head and back, while the underside is white. *R. limnocharis*, with a body length of at least 4.5 cm is the commonest. Two other smaller species seen less frequently are *R. pierrei* and *R. syhadrensis*.

Hiding under logs and fallen branches in the sal forest is another rarely seen terrestrial frog, *R. danieli*, which has a cinnamon-tan back and head, dark brown sides and dusky underparts

From the flat, tropical lowlands of the Terai at 150 m above sea level, the mountains rise ever higher, forced upward by tectonic pressure to culminate in icy 8000-m summits.

3. The Land

From Seabed to Mountain Range

Two great continental landmasses, one of them moving relentlessly toward the other over the past 60 million years, have produced one of the greatest collisions on earth. Originally situated in the Southern Hemisphere, the Indian subcontinent broke off from the continent of Gondwanaland and moved slowly north, at an estimated 10–11 cm per year. Movement did not cease when the Indian subcontinent reached the landmass of Eurasia, although it slowed. Today India still pushes, slowly but steadily, under the edge of the Eurasian plate, at a rate of about 5 cm per year.

The Sea of Tethys, an ocean once situated between the two continents, drained and shrank as the landmasses moved closer, until eventually it no longer existed. While this was happening the Eurasian landmass was also being forced upward. Alluvium, silt and coarse materials eroded from the young mountains by rivers — the Brahmaputra and Indus of India, and the Koshi and Gandaki of Nepal — were deposited on the floor of the shrinking ocean. This parent material was later compressed to form conglomerate quartzes, shales and micaceous sandstones.

Dawn — Narayani River

As a result of continued pressure, the edges of the Eurasian plate have buckled and crumpled. Three major uplifts have occurred. The first caused the Eurasian plate to rise, creating mountains in Tibet. The second, within the last five million years, created that huge massif, the Himalaya. After a period of rest, a third upheaval uplifted the former seabed, along with the edge of the present plains of northern India, to form the Siwalik Hills.

The Siwaliks form the first low undulation of Himalayan foothills. They lie parallel to the high mountains, extending east-west for 2400 km, but only 800 km of the range is included within the boundaries of Nepal. The bouldery, unstable, easily eroded coarse soil, and lack of surface water make the Siwaliks unsuitable for cultivation. Thus, the typical terracing which covers most hillsides throughout the rest of Nepal has not taken place. The range is named after a temple to Lord Shiva, in Hardwar, India.

THE PHYSIOGRAPHIC REGIONS OF NEPAL AND SOUTHERN TIBET

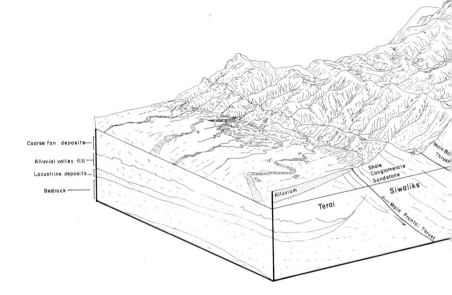

Two to three million years ago, when the Siwaliks were being formed, the Chitwan area was a lake which drained southward through what is now the Reu Valley. As the mountains rose this exit became blocked off. Today the Reu is the only major river which flows north from the Siwaliks and as a result of tectonic activity the valley has hot springs. The Chitwan area is now drained by the Rapti and Reu Rivers, which flow into the Narayạni River. This large waterway has since cut a narrow gorge through the Siwaliks to exit on their southern side at the sacred site of Tribeni. The Rapti and Reu are *duns* — broad, low-altitude valleys contained entirely within the Siwaliks. They are commonly known as the Inner Terai.

North of the Siwaliks are the Mahabharat mountains. Erosion of the Siwaliks and the Mahabharat Range has produced quantities of gravels and fine silt. Over the centuries these materials have filled the dun valleys, producing the rich, fertile soil which makes the Inner Terai suitable for agriculture. Most of the original lake-bed material is now buried, except for a small area near Tikoli.

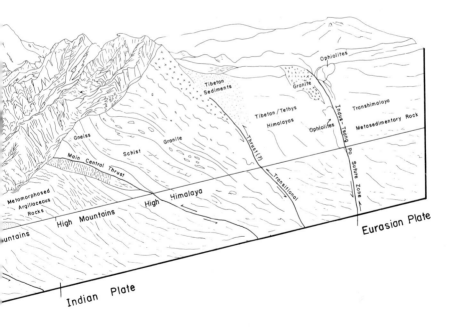

Collision of two continental plates has crumpled their edges and forced the land to rise, forming increasingly higher rows of mountains.

71

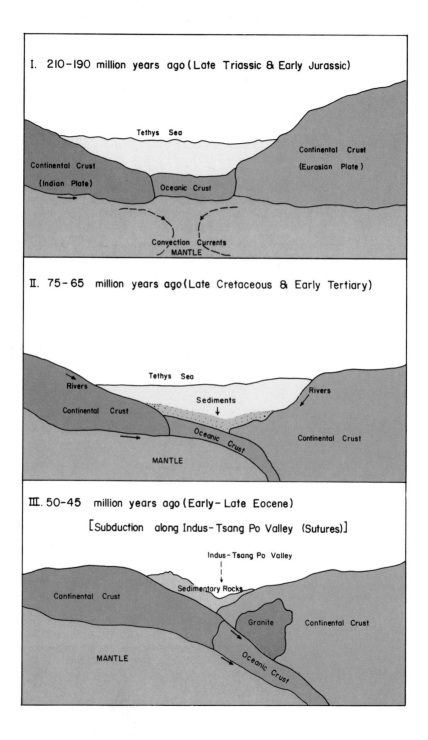

I. 210–190 million years ago (Late Triassic & Early Jurassic)

Tethys Sea

Continental Crust
(Eurasian Plate)

Continental Crust
(Indian Plate)

Oceanic Crust

Convection Currents
MANTLE

II. 75–65 million years ago (Late Cretaceous & Early Tertiary)

Tethys Sea

Rivers

Sediments

Rivers

Continental Crust

Oceanic Crust

Continental Crust

MANTLE

III. 50–45 million years ago (Early–Late Eocene)

[Subduction along Indus–Tsang Po Valley (Sutures)]

Indus–Tsang Po Valley

Sedimentary Rocks

Continental Crust

Granite

Continental Crust

MANTLE

Oceanic Crust

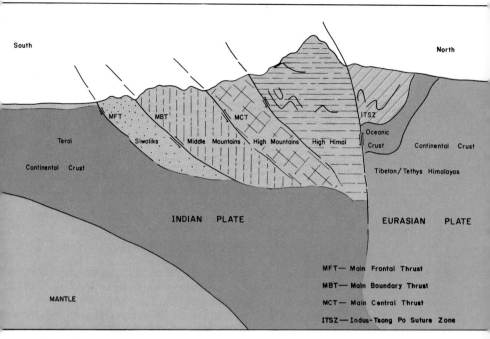

These four diagrams summarise the geological history of the Himalayan region.

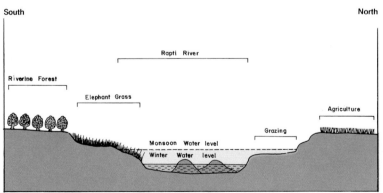

A cross-section of the Rapti River showing seasonal river levels.

Rivers, Hills and Valleys

Long and irregularly shaped, with a main east-west axis, Royal Chitwan National Park falls within latitude 27° north and longitude 84° east, in the Siwalik physiographic region of Nepal. More than half its boundaries are delineated by rivers — the Rapti forming its northern border, the Narayani its west, and the Reu marking part of the southern border. The Narayani, also known as the Kali Gandaki in its upper reaches, is the third largest river in Nepal. Several wooded islands in this river are included within the Park.

In Nepal the Siwalik range is known as the Churia Hills. In the Chitwan area parts of the Churias are also known as the Someshwar and Dauney Hills. The main Churia ridge commences at the western end of the Park between the Rapti and Reu rivers. Rising from their floodplains, it extends eastward to a height of over 600 m. The lower slopes of this range are gentle and dissected by many streams, but incline steeply at the top to the main ridge, which varies from a knife edge to a broad plateau.

The narrow, saw-backed range rising over 500 m on the south side of the Reu Valley, along the international border between Nepal and India, is called the Someshwar Hills, a name given by Gurkha soldiers who manned a fort there early last century. Steep, ravine-gouged slopes of the rugged Someshwar Hills form the southwestern boundary of the Park. West of the Narayani River, a small part of the similar, rugged terrain known as the Dauney Hills is also included in the Park.

From lower areas of the Park, averaging only 150 m in altitude, it is possible to see several 8000-metre peaks of the Himalaya, less than 100 km away in the north. The snowcapped mountains provide an impressive contrast to the tropical environment of the Park.

Grasslands and riverine forests along the floodplains are most favoured by large mammals. The sal forests in the hills are traversed by a few trails and roads used mainly by park staff and local people.

Sun, Wind and Rain

The climate of Chitwan is humid and warm for much of the year, but there are three quite distinct seasons — winter, a cool dry period; pre-monsoon, the hot dry time; and the monsoon, which is hot and wet.

During winter, which lasts from late October until about mid February, dry westerly winds bring low temperatures and low humidity. The cool, clear air allows good views of the Himalaya. December and January are the coldest months, when night temperatures fall to about 5° C and frosts sometimes occur. Fog forms in the valleys and during the early morning condenses as heavy dew. Dripping from trees and

The Rapti River in summer. Monsoon rains change a gentle, clear flow to a destructive, silt-laden flood.

other vegetation, it sounds much like rain. The cool, wet mist usually blankets the valleys until late morning, but once it has dispersed, afternoon temperatures often rise to 25° C. Winter storms, with low daytime temperatures, can be violent and unexpected. They are usually of short duration but produce enough rain to benefit vegetation.

The hot dry season begins from late February and is heralded by the shrieking call of the hawk cuckoo. The wind now comes from the southwest and shade temperatures climb steadily, peaking at more than 36° C in May. Nights are rarely cooler than 20° C. Pre-monsoon thunderstorms become more frequent in April and May. They are often accompanied by violent winds and hail and can damage crops, houses and trees. Rainfall is short and heavy. Hot and dust-laden, the air is hazy, obscuring the mountains but producing spectacular sunsets and sunrises.

With the arrival of the monsoon, usually about mid June, the showers and thunderstorms become increasingly frequent. By now the prevailing westerly winds of the dry season have swung southeast. Carrying moisture, they flow up from the Bay of Bengal and are forced to rise against the mountain barriers. As the air rises, it cools and the moisture condenses, to fall as torrential rain. Monsoon rains are not continuous and there are many dry spells.

The onset of monsoon rains reduces the temperature slightly from its April-May peak, but the weather is still hot. The heat, combined with high humidity, provides ideal conditions for the growth of moulds and fungi. July and August are the wettest months. By early October about 80 per cent of the park's annual 200 cm of rain has already fallen and the cool dry winter season soon begins again.

Scarlet-flowered simal trees colour the riverine forest along the banks of the Narayani River.

4. The Dynamics of Chitwan

A Changing Environment

The environment of Chitwan is not static but is dynamic with an everchanging mosaic of rivers, grassland, and forests. Two contrasting elements — water and fire — affect this environment, altering the course of plant succession and creating constant changes in vegetation patterns.

Water is both a life-giver and a destroyer. Abundant rains combined with warm temperatures promote rapid growth of vegetation, and flooding brings nutrient-rich silt. Too much water also causes great destruction. Torrential rains at higher altitudes swell rivers immensely. On reaching the Terai, the rivers overflow their banks, often changing course and devastating areas of well established vegetation.

When water levels recede in autumn, new sandbanks, islands and ponds are revealed. New areas are quickly colonised by grasses, the earliest plants in a succession. First to colonise is usually the grass *Saccharum spontaneum*, which eventually grows to 6 m. Its long runners creep out in a crisscrossing network, stabilising the sand and gathering nutrients for other species in the succession.

If the grassland remains undisturbed, trees progressively become established. The first are usually **shishoo** or **Indian rosewood** (*Dalbergia sissoo*) and **khair** or **cutch** (*Acacia catechu*), both of which help to stabilise the soil further, followed by the **simal** or **silk cotton tree** (*Bombax ceiba*).

Saccharum spontaneum, the first plant to colonise new sandbanks.

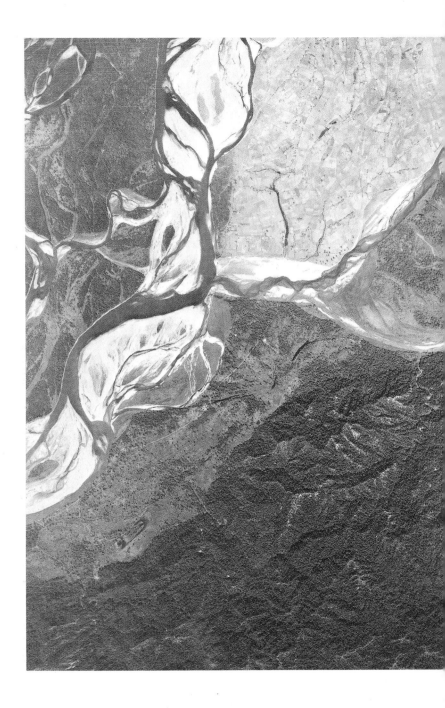

An aerial view of the Narayani, Rapti and Reu rivers clearly shows their changing paths over the years. The forested islands of the Narayani River (to left) are often totally submerged during monsoon floods.

The centuries-old practice of burning the grasslands discourages the invasion of trees.

Two other early colonisers of the grasslands, particularly along streambeds, are **bhelur** (*Trewia nudifora*) and *Ehretia laevis*. The leaves and fruit of bhelur are palatable to rhinos, which helps to spread this tree. Seeds passing unharmed through the rhino's digestive system are deposited with dung at rhino latrines, where they germinate. The rhino's digestive juices help to break down the seed's tough outer coat and thereby initiate the first stages in germination.

Shade provided by the first trees creates a more suitable environment for smaller herbs and shrubs and eventually a riverine type of forest dominates the grasslands. As the years pass, the changing soil structure supports an increasing variety of tree species. Eventually, where drainage is good, these are replaced by **sal** (*Shorea robusta*), which forms the climax forest seen covering the Siwalik Hills and other higher areas of the Park.

Fire, the other element affecting Chitwan, is an integral part of the ecology. Natural fires caused by lightning are possible, but for hundreds of years the aboriginal peoples have been burning the grasslands to maintain them for grazing and to retard the encroachment of forests. If left unburnt, the grasslands would become too dense, impeding their own growth but encouraging conditions suitable for the invasion of trees.

Many grasses are used traditionally by local people for house construction. Once the useful grasses have been cut, the remainder are burnt at random. The early fires do not spread far because the grass is still green. They are also contained by watercourses and clearings and the heavy dew at night. In March and April, when the grass is drier, the fires spread quickly, often fanned by afternoon breezes. Areas of riverine forest are sometimes burnt along with the grass, with many young trees being destroyed. Fires also spread to the sal forests, burning easily but slowly through the carpet of recently fallen dry leaves. The flames are not hot enough to damage mature trees.

The effect of fire is not as devastating to vegetation as might be imagined. What is not known is its effect on small mammals. Although burning through dry grassland at very high temperatures, the fires move quickly, raising ground temperatures only slightly. Mature trees are not affected and many seeds within the soil are not killed. Encouraged by moisture from spring showers, they germinate quickly on the newly burnt ground. Nevertheless, continued burning does seem to favour only fire-resistant trees such as simal and sal.

On most floodplains the water table is high and grasses produce new shoots within 2 weeks. Pre-monsoon showers accelerate growth, which often reaches 3 m by the time the monsoon rains set in. Tender new grass shoots are preferred by animals, as they provide a higher amount of protein. Since different areas of grassland are burnt at different times, enough old grass is left to provide cover and shelter. With the onset of the monsoon, the Park rapidly takes on a luxuriant green mantle again.

The present pattern of vegetation found in Chitwan is largely maintained by the annual floods and fires, but other, more subtle, changes are also occurring, mainly due to intervention by humans. These changes are not so easily measured or understood, except by further scientific research.

A Sea of Waving Grass

Thick, matted and almost impenetrable by humans, the grasslands contain over 70 different grass species. Known collectively as "elephant grass", some grow 6 m high in places. For wildlife, either big or small, they provide a bounty of food, cover and shelter.

The grasslands cover about 20 per cent of the Park. Some areas are derived from past agricultural settlements and others are the initial stages of plant succession on new alluvium deposits. Different species of grasses dominate specific areas, depending on the stage of plant succession and amount of surface water available.

The lowest terraces, near rivers, are those most prone to flooding and alteration during the monsoon. They are covered almost entirely (about

Khar (*Imperata cylindrica*), a short grass used for thatching, flourishes on ground which was previously farmed.

90 per cent) with the hardy coloniser *Saccharum spontaneum*. The next highest terraces, where a few trees may have already become established, are covered mainly with *Narenga porphyrocoma*, a dense species which grows in association with other *Saccharum* and *Themeda* species, *Phragmites karka* and *Typha elephantina*. Shorter grass species grow beneath the tall cover. Along the edges of streams and small lakes is a different association of tall *Arundo donax* and sedge species.

By the end of the monsoon most grasses have reached their maximum height, and flowering takes place until late November. Each species flowers at a different time, presenting its plume of minute red, yellow, white or purple flowers in a sea of feathery flags. After flowering, the stems harden and foliage becomes tough and coarse. As an adaptation against the following dry season, most of their food is transferred and stored in the roots, with little nourishment left in the leaves.

Khar (*Imperata cylindrica*), a grass used for thatching, only reaches about 2 m tall and is found mainly on areas which were once farmed. These were cut and burned regularly to provide building materials and grazing for stock, until the occupants were resettled in 1964. Where khar is still harvested, it continues to dominate, but recently the taller and more aggressive *Saccharum* species have started to take over. It is possible that removal of cultivation and grazing pressures have influenced the decline of *Imperata*.

Grass flower plumes.

Regrowth after burning is rapid. The change from charred stalks (right) to tall, impenetrable grassland (below) takes only a few months.

After burning, the grasslands appear blackened and charred, but closer scrutiny reveals a different picture. In moist hollows ferns push rapidly through the blackened soil. The tender, green fronds are collected by villagers and eaten as a vegetable. **Rhino thistle** (*Cirsium wallichii*), also grows quickly, taking advantage of the newly exposed soil and increased light.

Much of the grassland, particularly where it merges with riverine forest, is an open, savannah-type environment dotted with widely spaced simal trees which have survived the annual burning. In winter a parasitic mistletoe, *Dendropthoe falcata*, shows as dark patches amongst the bare, whorled branches of these tall, buttressed trees. In spring the simal are a mass of red flowers.

The Riverine Forest

Riverine forest, as its name implies, grows along streamsides and riverbanks; a bountiful resource, it covers about 7 per cent of the Park. It has a mixture of tall and medium-height trees with a thick understorey of tangled shrubs and herbs, the composition varying according to soil and availability of water. Recently colonised areas, such as the gravel islands in the Narayani River, are dominated by **shishoo** (*Dalbergia sissoo*) in moist places and along riverbanks, and **khair** (*Acacia catechu*) where it is drier. Pure stands of both these trees occur, often growing to 15 m in height.

The spiny, deciduous khair produces a crown of feathery greenery in spring, followed by cylindrical spikes of fragrant, pale cream flowers in May and June. From the flowers, long, straight pods form and ripen to a dark brown in November. Khair wood is used widely for making agricultural implements, wheels, oil crushers, rice pestles and for house frames; the seed pods make good cattle feed because of their high protein content. The other name for khair is "cutch", derived from the thick, syrupy black resin produced by boiling chips of khair heartwood. Cutch is used for dyeing, tanning and a range of medicines. A valuable gum can also be made from cutch and an extract is chewed with betel leaf to produce red spittle.

Shishoo is also deciduous and, like khair, is a legume. Between March and May short bunches of yellowish flowers appear. The long, flat seedpods ripen to a dark brown in winter and are blown from trees to be dispersed along the riverbanks by water. The pods eventually rot, releasing flat, kidney-shaped seeds which germinate and continue the colonisation of riverbanks. Shishoo wood has elasticity and strength and is used extensively for furniture. It is also a good fuel wood, and the leaves and twigs provide fodder for animals.

While flowering, simal trees attract many species of birds and insects

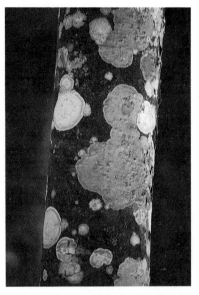

The spiny bark of a young simal and lichen-encrusted trunk of a bhelur tree are both distinctive.

which pollinate the fleshy red blossoms as they feed noisily on the nectar. Fallen blooms provide food for both domestic and wild animals. Immature flowers are sometimes used as a vegetable. When ripe, the long seedpods burst open, releasing smooth, oval seeds enveloped in a thick mass of long, silky white floss. The seeds provide a nourishing food for cattle, and the white floss, known as kapok, is used worldwide to stuff cushions, pillows and mattresses.

As an adaptation against browsing animals, the trunks and branches of young simal trees are covered with conical spines, giving a warty appearance. Some local people believe these spines can house evil spirits and that they are used in hell to prick the bodies of sinners. As the tree grows bigger, its trunk thickens and the spines are eventually replaced by smooth, light-coloured bark.

Bhelur (*Trewia nudiflora*) has smooth, grey bark which is usually blotched with conspicuous patches of white and orange lichens. The fresh new leaves of this deciduous tree emerge in spring along with the flowers. The male flowers hang in long, pale green clusters; by contrast, female flowers are single on stout stalks, and without petals. The wood is used for rough planking, drums and carving, and the leaves as fodder for domestic animals.

Tanki (*Bauhinia malabarica*), another important tree, is recognised by its rounded, bilobal leaves with 7–9 veins radiating from the base. The wood is used as fuel, and the tender young flowers are eaten as a vegetable.

There is a diversity of flowers among the riverine forest trees; simal or kapok (top left), "flame of the forest" (top right), mitho nim or curry-leaf tree (left) and male flowers of the bhelur tree (below).

Flowers of the tanki tree (top left) are used as a vegetable. Shrubs of *Caryopteris odorata* (top right), sweet-scented *Clerodendrum viscosum* (below) and starry *Coffea benghalensis* (right) border the riverine forest and form a tangled understorey.

When the "flame of the forest" or palash (*Butea monosperma*) comes into flower in March, its spectacular colour competes with that of the simal. Keeled blossoms crown the tree in a mass of orange, appearing in tight bunches at the end of leafless twigs and occasionally from the dark, crooked trunks. Long, yellowish-grey pods form quickly and ripen between May and June, releasing a single seed while still on the tree. A coarse brown fibre obtained from the bark of the roots is used for caulking boats; the wood is used mainly for constructing wells and water scoops.

In the shaded understorey, a variety of shrubs provide splashes of colour. White, star-shaped flowers of *Coffea benghalensis* appear on low, spindly, leafless bushes in February. In March the curry-leaf tree or mitho nim (*Murraya koenigii*) produces bunches of small white flowers at the ends of branchlets, along with new leaves. The pungent-smelling leaflets are used in parts of India to flavour curries. In some places dursia (*Colebrookea oppositifolia*) forms almost the entire understorey. The soft, slightly furry leaves and fuzzy white flower spikes of this member of the mint family are unpalatable to animals, allowing it to grow unchecked.

Dursia (*Colebrookea oppositifolia*).

Bhanti (*Clerodendron viscosum*) is another common shrub, noticeable in spring by its strongly scented white blossoms. *Caryopteris odorata*, a tall, woody herb, and *Pogostemon bengalensis*, with mint-smelling leaves, both have spikes of purplish-blue flowers. At ground level is the ever persistent *Ageratum conyzoides* with its small, fuzzy, white or blue flowers.

Although most riverine forest trees are deciduous, there are some evergreens. **Jamun** (*Syzygium cumini*) often forms large stands along streambanks or other damp sites, its thick, dark green foliage casting deep shadows which inhibit the growth of understorey plants. Clusters of small, sweet-scented white flowers, with masses of prominent stamens, appear in early spring. The dark-coloured, shiny, round fruit has succulent pink flesh which is edible, giving rise to the jamun tree's other name, Java or black plum. The wood makes good fuel and is also used for well curbs, buildings and agricultural implements, while the leaves are used for fodder.

Other common evergreen species are *Litsea monopetala*, a member of the laurel family, and pipal and kabhro, both Ficus species. **Pipal** (*Ficus religiosus*) is considered sacred, as it was under one of these trees that Buddha received enlightenment. For this reason the wood is never used as fuel but the leaves provide excellent fodder for elephants. **Kabhro** (*F. lacor*) leaves are also used extensively for fodder. The bark is used for medicines and rope is made from its fibres. Both pipal and kabhro start life as epiphytes, from seeds carried in bird droppings. Deposited in the forks of trees, they germinate in the moisture-laden leaf litter. The new seedling sends down roots, which eventually enlarge and strangle the host tree. The figs are important food for birds and animals.

Another evergreen, **sano panheli** (*Mallotus philippensis*), is easily recognised in winter by its ripe fruit — clusters of three-lobed capsules covered in bright, rust-red powder. A silk dye is obtained from this powder and it is also used for medicines and in some Hindu festivals. The pale yellow flowers appear around August, borne on separate male and female trees. The male flowers, growing in clusters on long spikes, are particularly conspicuous; the female flowers occur singly on short spikes.

A common shrub growing in the shade of evergreen trees is **latikel** (*Citrus medica*). It has strongly scented white flowers and dark green leaves which have a distinctive citrus smell when crushed. The fruit is a small red berry.

Several species of vines entwine the trees, many of them with vicious thorns. A common one is the leguminous *Acacia concinna*, with reddish flowers which whiten as they age. The thornless *Vallaris solanaceae* is less vicious. It has soft, dull green leaves and produces oval green pods suspended on long stalks.

Powder from the ripe fruits of sano panheli (*Mallotus philippensis*) is used in a silk dye and medicines.

Sal Forests

Tall and stately, with straight trunks standing row after row, the sal tree (*Shorea robusta*) clothes higher areas and hills, covering almost 70 per cent of the Park. Although deciduous, sal is never entirely leafless, its new leaves emerging in early April when most of the old ones are still falling. At this time the forests are a magnificent sight, the crowns of trees smothered in masses of small, creamy flowers which scent the hot, dry air.

Averaging 30 to 40 m in height, sal is one of the most important trees of Nepal. Being extremely hard and durable, the timber is used for railway sleepers, bridges and houses. A white resin, tapped from the trunks, is used as incense during religious festivals. Large areas of forest were cut in the past, and are still being cut today in unprotected areas, resulting in over-exploitation of the species.

The large, pointed oval leaves are often pinned together with fine slivers of bamboo to make plates for use at marriage feasts and other festivals. Sal trees growing outside the Park near villages are frequently lopped so much to provide bedding and fodder for domestic animals that the result is a tall trunk devoid of foliage, except for a few bunches and tufts of leaves near the top. These trees are hardly recognisable as the same leafy giants within the Park.

Sal forests. The sal tree produces masses of tiny, sweet-scented flowers in April. Where the forest canopy is broken, grasses flourish; elsewhere they are sparse and mixed with phoenix palms (right), small shrubs and herbs.

Even the seeds do not escape, as they are crushed to produce an oil for use in lamps and medicines. Contained within fleshy oval fruits, which have five long wings, the ripe seeds are a conspicuous sight in May, hanging from the trees in large brown bunches.

Unlike the riverine forests, pure stands of sal forest have little undergrowth, particularly in places where the canopy is unbroken. Thinly spaced grasses and a few small herbs, shrubs and scattered phoenix palms are the main groundcover. Here the dominant grass species, *Themeda caudata*, grows to only 2 m. In areas where the canopy is broken, allowing more light in, it will grow to 6 m.

On flat ground a common lower canopy species is **tatari** (*Dillenia pentagyna*), a tree with large, pointed oblong leaves crowded toward the ends of branches. On young trees they are very large and distinctive. Like sal, tatari is deciduous but never quite leafless. Around March, large, fragrant yellow flowers appear, bunched on the thick, almost leafless twigs. These produce succulent, orange-yellow fruit which are edible, but laxative.

Fringe areas of sal forest, where it merges with grassland or riverine forest, have a denser understorey and greater variety of species. Huge vines of **bhorla** (*Bauhinia vahlii*) form twisted, contorted ropes around and between trees, smothering their crowns with large, twin-lobed, butterfly-like leaves. Ropes are made from the bark of bhorla and the leaves are used for sun and rain shields and to make plates. In contrast to those of other trees, the new leaves of **kusum** (*Schleichera oleosa*) are bright red when they first emerge in March and April, creating a vivid splash of colour within the overall spring green. The green, egg-shaped fruit of this tree has a pleasant acidic taste and is considered a delicacy by local people.

Another fruit favoured by the villagers is **amala** (*Phyllanthus emblica*). Sour tasting and greenish-coloured, amala is similar in appearance to a gooseberry, hence its English name, "Indian gooseberry". It ripens in winter and is either eaten raw or used to make pickles. Wood from the moderate-sized, deciduous amala is sacred because of its association with the gods Shiva and Vishnu. A durability in water makes it good for constructing wells, furniture and agricultural tools.

Three species of *Terminalia* are commonly found associated with sal. **Asna** or **saj** (*T. alata),* a tall tree with bark resembling crocodile skin, produces a profusion of small, creamy coloured flowers on erect spikes in spring, along with new leaves. The hard fruit, with its five broad, striated wings is often found on the ground where it has fallen before ripening. **Barro** (*T. belerica*) produces a fruit which is a valuable source of commercial myrobalan — a substance used for tanning and dyeing. It is also a favourite food of deer, monkeys and domestic animals. Unlike the winged fruit of asna, that of barro is fleshy, with smooth, velvety-

In fringe areas of the sal forest huge vines twist around and between trees as they reach upward to the light.

Young tatari (*Dillenia pentagyna*) trees with their large leaves are a distinctive understorey species in flat areas of sal forest.

Ageratum conyzoides (above) seems to have flowers in all seasons, but other herbs, such as the ground orchid *Eulophia explanata* (left) need spring and summer warmth to bring them into bloom.

grey skin. The third species, **harro** (*T. chebula*), is economically important because its hard, distinctively five-ribbed, yellow-brown fruit is the source of commercial black myrobalan.

Many other trees found associated with sal have some local use. *Holarrhena pubescens*, a small tree known as **dudhey**, has a rough, flaky brown bark used to prepare an antidysentery medicine. The bark is also powdered and rubbed on to a patient's back to alleviate dropsy.

Haldu (*Adena cordifolia*), a large deciduous tree with a thick, spreading crown, is common in lower fringes of the sal forest. Its trunk, often fluted and buttressed at the base, is considered the best for making dugout canoes. Ungulates frequently browse the heart-shaped leaves, often causing considerable damage to young trees. An associated tree, **phaldu** (*Mitragyna parviflora*), is similar in appearance in many respects. Both belong to the family Rubiaceae.

The succulent yellow fruit of **khamari** (*Gmelina arborea*) is an important source of food for bats and birds. They in turn help to disperse the seeds. In February and March, khamari trees produce masses of tubular, yellow-brown blossoms which fall quickly, carpeting the ground in gold.

Along ridges of the Siwaliks, **bhalayo** or **marking-nut trees** (*Semecarpus anarcardium*) are quite common. They can be seen on the walk to Black Rock, above Tiger Tops Jungle Lodge. The large, oval leaves are shed in early spring and new leaves appear in May. When ripe in winter, the shiny black fruit rests in a bright orange, fleshy, cup-like receptacle. It produces a dark, corrosive juice which is used as an ink and in the preparation of a variety of medicines. An acrid gum, exuded when the rough bark is cut, is also used in medicines.

Shaded, moist watercourses and gullies descending from the hills support evergreen vegetation. **Damai phul** (*Ardisia solanaceae*) produces attractive pink waxy flowers throughout the year, though more profusely in March and April. When ripe in winter, the pea-sized black fruit is usually full of pink juice. Bushes of *Phlogacanthus thyrsiflorus* display large spikes of rust-brown flowers in spring, and in favourable sites bamboo forms dense thickets.

Phlogacanthus thyrsiflorus prefers shaded gullies.

On higher, dry ridges of the Siwaliks, the sal is mixed with **chir pine** (*Pinus roxburghii*). Here the pines are often taller than the sal, but neither species grows densely. Apart from short grasses, the forest floor is almost bare.

Rivers, Lakes and Swamps

The aquatic environment of Chitwan is an important part of the ecosystem, for it supports a variety of plant and animal communities. Apart from the three major rivers, there are numerous small streams flowing down from the Siwalik Hills, as well as several small lakes, known as *tals*. Tals are oxbow lakes formed when a river changes course and cuts off part of its old bed, leaving a long, narrow body of water. Scattered throughout the grasslands are other low-lying areas which provide permanently wet, swampy habitats.

Aquatic vegetation growing in these places supports many small creatures such as fish, molluscs, crustaceans, amphibians and insect larvae. These in turn are food for the many waterfowl and small mammals which find food and cover among the long grasses and reeds around the edges. The lakes and swamps are also the favourite haunts of mugger crocodiles, their grass and sandy banks providing good basking and nesting sites.

Oxbow lakes within the grasslands provide a rich aquatic environment.

The water hyacinth — a beautiful but pernicious scourge.

An introduced water hyacinth, *Eichhornia crassipes,* has infested many of Chitwan's tals. Brought to India from South America as an ornamental plant, it has spread throughout the subcontinent and now threatens these lakes. The water hyacinth has the ability to multiply itself 60,000 times in only 8 months. By covering the water surface it cuts out light. This changes the ecology, making it difficult for fish, plant and animal species to survive. The weed is periodically removed from the water by Park staff, but seems almost impossible to eradicate.

This scorpion's sting is very painful but not fatal to humans.

5. Base of the Pyramid: Invertebrates

The wildlife of Chitwan can be visualised as a pyramid, with tigers
occupying the apex and the invertebrates forming the base. During the
cooler winter months insects are not noticeable, but with the onset of
pre-monsoon rains their numbers escalate and they become obvious.
Tender new leaves, flowers and fruits provide food for new generations
of insects and their larvae. Many of these creatures are eaten by larger
invertebrates such as spiders, praying mantises and centipedes. Birds,
reptiles, amphibians and small mammals eat the larger predatory
invertebrates and in turn also become prey to even larger animals in an
increasingly higher pyramid of complex life-support systems.

The Smallest Invertebrates

Smallest, usually unnoticed, and least attractive to humans, the aphids,
ticks and mites obtain their nourishment by sucking juices. Aphids are
well known insect pests which pierce plant tissues and suck out the sap.
An ability to reproduce both sexually and asexually leads to rapid
increases in aphid numbers in a very short time. Some mites also
parasitise plants; others have animal hosts, as do the larger ticks.
Attached firmly by means of specialised mouthparts, ticks can suck
many times their own body weight of blood from their host until their
highly distensible bodies become swollen and pealike. These arachnids
carry diseases and can cause discomfort. Bites can become infected if the
animal's body is pulled off and the head is left behind.

To reproduce, female mosquitoes must suck blood. The males feed on
plant sap and nectar. Most mosquitoes in Chitwan are harmless, but
females of some species of the *Anopheles* and *Culex* genera are carriers
of malaria and encephalitis. Mosquito eggs are laid in slow-moving or
stagnant water and the aquatic larvae feed on microscopic plants and
animals. The notorious whining sound of mosquitoes is caused by their
wing vibrations, males having a different frequency and pitch from
females. Although the spraying of breeding grounds during the 1950s
had eradicated malaria from the Terai by 1960, several species have
since become resistant to DDT. Incidences of malaria and encephalitis
have increased in the last few years.

At night, fireflies are obvious when they flash their greenish light, in
an intermittent, will-o'-the-wisp fashion, to attract partners. To avoid
confusion, each species of this tiny beetle has its own specific glow,
produced by abdominal glands. These glands contain luciferin, which
generates light when-mixed with air. The intensity and timing of the
glow is controlled by the insect itself.

In spring and summer, weird and wonderful caterpillars munch their way to maturity.

Large, colourful locusts (*Schistocera* spp.) whirr busily through grasslands.

Masters of mimicry, stick and leaf insects often remain unnoticed as they feed on vegetation. The stick insect's long green or brown, twig-like body is almost impossible to detect unless it moves. Even then it usually just drops to the ground and remains as if lifeless. Amongst leaves the flattened body and legs of a leaf insect provide equally good camouflage.

The omnivorous praying mantis is also a mimic. With forelegs folded in a prayer-like attitude, this predator remains motionless until some unsuspecting insect passes by. Then, striking swiftly, the praying mantis takes its victim by surprise. Praying mantises found among shrubbery and trees are green and blend with their surroundings. Others are sandy-coloured and textured, rendered almost invisible on the side of a termite nest or sandy path.

Within the pale, fluted termite mounds that abound in Chitwan's forests are extraordinary social organisations comparable to those of ants and bees. Each termite colony has workers, soldiers, and reproductive members. Soldier and worker termites are sterile and wingless. Fertile termites grow wings and swarm at certain times of the year, often after pre-monsoon rain. They burst from the ground and rise in clouds as they seek mates. Most are eaten by birds before they fly far, but mated pairs which survive move away to form a new royal cell. The female becomes a bloated queen, up to 12 cm long, producing millions of eggs during her long lifespan. Because of her size, the queen is imprisoned within the colony, along with her wasp-sized king. Both are

A predator of other insects, the praying mantis comes in different colours, depending on its habitat.

Swarms of fertile, winged termites leave the mound to mate and start a new nest.

fed by the workers. Termites eat dead wood, digesting the cellulose with special protozoans and bacteria living in their intestines.

The ubiquitous ants also live in colonies, usually underground or, in the case of black tree ants, in spherical nests attached to tree branches. Some species of red ants live in leaves glued together. The ever-busy worker ants are sterile, wingless females. At certain times during the year, fertile offspring grow wings and swarm. After mating, the males die and surviving females become the queens of new ant colonies.

Spiders, Scorpions, Beetles and Bees

On the forest floor, dung beetles, earwigs, centipedes, millipedes, spiders, slugs and snails forage for food in the leaf litter. The cylindrical, segmented millipedes eat decaying vegetation, whereas the predatorial, flat-bodied centipedes prefer to dine on insects and spiders. Poison injected when centipedes bite is sufficient to kill prey and can also cause severe pain to humans.

Centipedes and spiders are predators of other insects and small animals. Although the centipede can inflict a painful bite, the fearsome-looking bird-eating spider (below) is harmless to humans. The leaf bug (*Dalader acuticosta*) tries to avoid detection by predators with a leaf shape and cryptic colouring.

The flat, pouch-like honeycombs of wild bees are a favourite food of sloth bears.

Of all spiders, the bird-eating spider is among the largest and longest lived. These hairy arachnids, with a leg span of more than 15 cm, do not spin webs but live under bark and leaves on the forest floor. They either search actively for prey or just sit and wait for it. The large size of the bird-eating spider allows it to attack small reptiles, mammals and birds, but it is harmless to humans.

Other spiders live in trees or shrubs and weave intricate webs to trap flying prey. In most spider species the females are larger than the males. Only the females are capable of spinning webs and the males' only function is to mate. Once this duty is performed, the male is either eaten by his partner or dies of exhaustion.

Male scorpions are also eaten by their partners after mating. The female scorpion gives birth to live young and carries the brood on her back until they become independent, usually after their first moult. During winter, scorpions are not often seen as they stay hidden in crevices and under rocks, but in summer the monsoon rains often flush them out of their hiding-places. Although the neurotoxic poison of the species found in Chitwan is not potent enough to cause death, the sting is extremely painful.

Leafy foliage and crevices of tree trunks host a number of bugs, beetles, borers and weevils. The large, bright coloured, **red cotton bug** (*Dysdercus cingulatus*) is very common and noticeable in spring, particularly when several of them cover the fallen floss and seeds of simal. The eggs of this bug cause the bubbly galls on bhelur leaves.

Male cicadas shrill to attract mates while hornets and wasps hover in search of flowers and fruit, or an unwary spider. Multicoloured grasshoppers cling to grass stems and brilliant damselflies and dragonflies hover over water and reeds. A variety of bees fill the air with a persistent hum as they gather nectar and pollen. Flat and pouch-like, the honeycombs of the **common bee** (*Apis dorsata*) festoon trees like empty Christmas stockings, their surface darkened by a seething mass of the insects. A smaller bee, *Apis indica*, also makes its combs in the forest and is sometimes domesticated and kept in wooden hives by villagers.

Leeches

When pre-monsoon showers break the hot dry weather of April and May, terrestrial leeches start appearing after spending winter underground. These infamous, bloodsucking, slug-like creatures have an uncanny sense of direction when it comes to homing in on humans and other warm-blooded creatures. They stretch out from damp leaf litter, grasses and leaves like hundreds of waving tentacles, waiting for an opportunity to latch themselves on to a victim. Measuring about 2 cm, with slightly flattened brown to black bodies when flaccid, leeches move by bringing one end of their body up to the other in a series of loops. The back end has a vacuum sucker, with which it grips its host; the other end is a mouth with sharp teeth. An anticoagulant, injected as the leech bites, prevents blood from clotting.

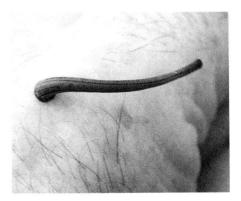

A leech — attached and ready for a meal.

Once a leech has attached itself, usually first noticed by a sudden itching, it is probably best left to drink its fill and drop off when ready. Leeches can be removed with salt or ashes, or by burning with a match or cigarette, but the wound will still bleed. Although unsightly, a leech bite is not usually harmful as leeches do not transmit disease. Nonetheless, care should be taken to not let the wound become infected. Once a leech has had a good meal, it does not feed again for months. Mammals are not the only hosts. Some leeches are aquatic, feeding on fish and other water animals; others are found on invertebrates such as snails and worms.

Butterflies and Moths

In contrast to leeches, butterflies are a delight. Almost 600 species have been recorded in Nepal so far, with representatives from all families except two from South America. As with the birds, this high number is due to Nepal's widely varying altitude, topography, and geographic position. About 150 species of butterfly are found in Chitwan. Most are tropical Oriental butterflies but there are a few Palearctic species such as the **dark clouded yellow** (*Colias fieldii*), **painted lady** (*Vanessa cardui*), **Indian red admiral** (*Vanessa indica*), **large cabbage white** (*Pieris brassicae*), and **peablue** (*Lamipides boeticus*).

Butterflies have definite seasons when they are most prolific. Some species are found in one season but not in another. For Chitwan, the best time to see them is from early March through to November, although a few are seen throughout the winter. Spring butterflies start appearing in March and are replaced in early May by pre-monsoon species. Summer species are seen later during the monsoon and post-monsoon period of October and November.

Strong-smelling objects such as animal dung, rotting fruit and dead animals are often attractive to butterflies. They also have a wide variety of preferred habitats. The males of some species often congregate on patches of damp ground near jungle streams or in riverbeds where they suck up moisture. It is not known whether this is a form of social behaviour or whether they collect in a particular place because the fare is tastier or better than in another.

Camouflage and mimicry are common among Nepal's butterflies. Many species with bright upper sides, such as the **orange oakleaf** (*Kallima inachus*), have brown markings on their undersides which allow them to masquerade as leaves once they fold their wings. The forest-dwelling **evening browns** (*Melanitis* species) are also almost impossible to see when they settle among dead leaves. Other species have different forms in different seasons. In the dry season the **peacock**

Protection from predators is important. In the dry season, a leaf shape and pattern camouflage the peacock pansy (above). The bright colours and strong markings carried by the common tiger (right), yellow pansy (below left) and rose windmill (below right) warn that their taste is not as good as their appearance.

pansy (*Precis almana*) not only has a leaf pattern but also a leaf shape which it lacks in the wet season.

Imitation of other butterflies, particularly those distasteful to predators, is another form of defence. The **common rose** (*Pachliopta aristolochiae*) and **red-bodied swallowtail butterflies** (*Atrophaneura* species) have irregularly shaped wings with bright red and white markings to warn predators against touching them. Their colour and wing shape are mimicked by other swallowtails (*Papilio* species). The bright reds and yellows of the **common jezebel** (*Delias eucharis*) and the **red-breasted jezebel** (*Delias hyparet*) also act as a warning. They are mimicked by other species, as are the extremely tough and unpalatable **tiger butterflies** (*Danaus* species).

A description of all the butterflies found in Chitwan is not possible here, but the families to which they belong have common characteristics. The variety within this framework is an endless kaleidoscope of colour, size and shape.

Generally, swallowtails (Papilionidae) are the largest and most brightly-coloured butterflies; some have tailed hindwings. The whites Pieridae are medium-sized butterflies with white or pale yellow ground colour and black, red or orange markings which are formed from waste products of metabolism in the larval stage. Small blue or iridescent green, copper or gold butterflies, with fine tails or hairs on their hindwings, will probably be members of the blues (Lycaenidae), a very large family. Other small, brightly patterned butterflies, occasionally with tails, are more likely to be "Punches and Judies" (Nemeobiidae).

An Indian fritillary is attracted to a patch of wet ground.

The boldly brown-and-white-patterned common sailer, a member of the Nymphalidae family, is a strong flier which ranges from the Terai to 3000 m.

Nepal has only one species of the family Amathusiidae, the **common duffer** (*Discophora sondaica*), and this is found in Chitwan. This large, dark coloured butterfly likes deep jungle habitats and is often seen flying at dusk.

The browns (Satyridae) are another shade-loving family of small to medium-sized butterflies. Usually dull brown or orange, with very thin antennae, the browns fly weakly, very close to the ground.

A slow, lazy flight, making them easy to catch, is the hallmark of tigers and crows (Danaidae). These medium to large, boldly marked butterflies are extremely tough and have no need for speed as they are protected from predators by their unpleasant taste.

Another very large family, the skippers (Hesperiidae), has generally small, dull-coloured members with pointed wings. Skippers usually have very rapid flight and prefer shady places.

The Nymphalidae family is perhaps the most varied in regard to wing shape and size. Its brightly coloured members are strong fliers and most like sun and flowers.

The world's largest moth, the **atlas moth** (*Attacus atlas*), which occurs throughout Asia, is also found in Chitwan. It prefers open places such as the Park boundaries. Males of this pale, brown-patterned species have a wingspan of more than 20 cm. The smaller females have a distinct scent to attract males. To help detect this scent, males have large antennae which are feathery to increase their surface area. Adult atlas moths do not live long as they have non-functional mouth parts and cannot feed. Males die as soon as they have mated and females as soon as they have laid their eggs.

Chitwan has many other species of moths, but little is known about them.

Darter.

Iora.

Black-backed forktail.

More than half of Nepal's birds have recorded in Royal Chitwan National

Purple gallinule.

Little egret.

White-backed vultures.

6. Birds of The Park

Nepal lies in a region where two biogeographic realms of Asia overlap
— the Palearctic to the north and the Oriental to the south. The flora
and fauna of the high Himalaya, in the Palearctic realm, are similar to
that of Europe and North Asia; in the low-altitude southern regions they
are dominated by tropical and subtropical species of the Oriental realm.
This overlap of two of the world's biotic provinces has endowed Nepal
with over 800 species of birds, almost one-tenth of those found in the
world. Over half of these have been recorded in the Royal Chitwan
National Park.

Chitwan, with its dense forests, grasslands, rivers, swamps and lakes,
provides a multitude of habitats for birds. Each provides a different type
of food and shelter. Even within the same habitat, different birds feed
selectively, minimising competition for food. The Park is a paradise for
birds and birdwatchers alike.

Many birds are regarded as residents because they live in the Park all
year round; others visit only in summer, often to breed. Another group
are the winter visitors which descend from mountainous regions to
spend the cold months in a more hospitable climate. Migratory birds
also use the Park during spring and autumn when resting on their
journeys to northern breeding grounds or southern wintering areas.

With well over 400 birds recorded in Chitwan, it is not feasible to
describe them all in this handbook. Excellent books on Nepal's birds are
available for anyone wishing to make positive identification (see Further
Reading). The birds mentioned here are those most likely to be seen by
visitors.

Grassland and Forest-Edge Birds

Possibly the most spectacular of all Chitwan's birds is the **common
peacock**. His brilliant plumage and magnificent tail, particularly when it
is erected into a great circular fan during courtship displays, are an
impressive sight. In spite of his long, trailing tail, the peacock often flies
into tall trees, announcing his presence with a loud, trumpeting call.
During the mating season in February, this polygamous pheasant will
have a harem of four or five hens. Groups of the comparatively drab,
grey-brown females are often disturbed in grassy areas near forest edges
as they search for insects, small snakes and geckos, fruits or green
shoots.

Colourful **red jungle fowl** are also frequently disturbed as they search
forest edges for insects and seeds. Both males and females look and

sound like domestic fowls, calling early in the morning and at dusk near their roosting places.

Dozens of small birds inhabit areas of grassland that are being slowly colonised by tree species. While some are inconspicuous, others are immediately noticeable. Groups of brilliantly coloured bee-eaters wheel in graceful arcs as they pursue and snap up flying insects. The **chestnut-headed bee-eater** usually hunts from fairly high in trees; the **green bee-eater** prefers bushes and shrubs in open country. The **blue-tailed bee-eater** favours areas near streams, skimming back and forth over the water, and nesting in holes in banks.

Perching on tall grass stems for a better view, the inquisitive **red-capped babbler** is unmistakable with its dark rufous crown, white face and distinctive sharp bill. This species and its earthy-brown cousins, the **jungle babbler** and **striated babbler**, are the most common representatives of several babblers found in Chitwan. Babblers are generally drab-coloured birds with strong, sharp bills adapted to a diet of insects, vegetable and animal matter. Although at times secretive, they tend to be gregarious and amazingly vocal if alarmed. Groups of jungle babblers often move noisily through shrubbery or along the ground, chattering and babbling as they bounce along with their tails flopping. Striated babblers have similar habits but prefer tall grass and marshy areas.

Red-whiskered and **red-vented bulbuls** also seem to like each other's company and often perch together on the tops of bushes or tall grass. These slim, dark birds, with semi-crested heads, are very common in the Park.

Prinias are another genus well represented in open, sunny areas where grassland and forest meet. Four species — the **grey-capped, yellow-bellied, ashy** and **Hodgson's prinias** — are all common resident birds. They are all small, and generally light tan in colour, except Hodgson's prinia, a sociable species which has grey and white toning.

Dense, matted grasses are favoured by two species of bustard-quails: the **button quail** and the **common bustard-quail**. When disturbed, they tend to rise explosively into the air and fly a short distance before settling again. The button quail is distinguished from the common bustard-quail by its yellow legs. Both resemble the common or grey quail but are smaller. Bustard-quails differ from true quails by not having a hind toe. Other unusual features are that the females are more colourful than the males and it is the latter who incubate and raise the young, while the females choose other partners and breed again.

The **black partridge**, a much bigger and darker bird, is common in the same habitat. The male has a black head, white cheeks and a chestnut collar. When flushed from its haunts, the black partridge flies close to the ground in a straight line.

While driving along Park roads, visitors will often see the **large**

(Top) A peacock displays his magnificent tail during the courtship dance to attract a harem.

(Above) Blue-tailed bee-eaters.

(Right) The red-whiskered bulbul is distinguished from other bulbuls by its white chin and red cheek patch.

coucal, or **crow pheasant** as it hunts amongst grass and reeds for other small birds or mammals and nests to rob of eggs. About the size of a crow, this handsome member of the cuckoo family is black with chestnut wings. Its close relative, the **small coucal**, has identical colouring except for a pale rufous tip to its tail. Usually solitary, the small coucal often perches on grass or reed stalks near water where it watches for grasshoppers, the basis of its diet.

The **black-headed shrike** likes to perch on top of bushes in more open areas. A long tail, rufous back, black head and pale breast make this bird distinctive. Its short, hooked bill is used for ripping apart prey such as small reptiles and young birds. In Nepal, the mandibles of the black-headed shrike are used by some people to feed rice to 6 months-old babies in a special "rice-feeding ceremony" to assure them of speech and wisdom later in life.

Small and robin-like, bush chats also perch on grass stalks or tops of bushes, occasionally flicking their tails and wings or darting out to catch insects. Three common species, the **pied**, the **collared** and the **white-tailed bush chats**, all have black, white and brown colouring which makes them difficult to tell apart except at close range.

Colonies of what may appear to be female house sparrows inhabiting marshy grasslands are more likely to be **baya weavers**. In summer, males sport a bright yellow cap and upper breast; otherwise they are only distinguished from sparrows by a larger bill and heavier black streaking on the back. The males of these interesting finches build long,

A collared bush chat watches for passing insects from the top of a bush.

retort-shaped nests, often starting many but only completing those which a female occupies. During nest-building there is a lot of noise, with each bird stealing grass from other nests being built. The **black-throated weaver** is similar to the baya weaver but slightly smaller and has a darker band of upper breast feathers. Being seed-eaters, weaver birds often raid grain fields adjacent to the Park.

Munias, which belong to the same family as weavers and sparrows, are also fairly common grassland residents. The **black-headed munia** and the **spotted munia** are two species seen frequently, the latter particularly where the grassland mixes with sal forest. They are small, gregarious birds with thick pointed bills typical of seed-eaters.

Flying over grasslands and forests as they chase airborne insects, **crested swifts** and **alpine swifts** can be recognised by their long, pointed wings which extend beyond their tails. They resemble swallows, but instead of having the latter's graceful flight, swifts move with a rapid fluttering. A streamlined bird, the crested swift has a long, wire-like tail and an unmistakable erect crest when it perches. Its nest, only a shallow saucer built on to a horizontal branch, has the egg glued into it.

Forest Birds

Forest-dwellers far outnumber grassland species, but because of dense vegetation many species can be difficult to locate and identify. The hornbills, noisy parakeets and pigeons are exceptions.

Hornbills are resident in Chitwan but are becoming rare elsewhere because extensive deforestation has destroyed many nesting trees. Their nesting is a strange routine. With help from the male, the female walls herself up inside a hole in a tree, using droppings, leaves, mud and pieces of sticky fig. A narrow slit, just big enough for a beak to pass through, is left so that the male can feed his mate while she incubates the eggs. When the chicks are about 2 weeks old the female comes out and the nest is resealed. Both partners then feed the young through the slit until they are old enough to leave the nest. The same nesting hole is often used on successive occasions.

Smallest of the three hornbills, the **grey hornbill** has only a small casque and an awkward-looking, undulating flight with the body held horizontal. **Pied hornbills** and **giant hornbills** are both black and white, but the former is much smaller, with a black neck. Pairs or small parties of this wary bird often feed in the tops of fruiting trees, their tails hanging down when they rest. The giant hornbill has a white neck and a huge beak topped with a large, flattened, yellow casque. When flying, its splayed wing feathers make a noisy, puffing sound.

If the four species of noisy, bright green parakeets which are resident in the Park are difficult to tell apart, then the pigeons are perhaps more so. Plump and fast flying, the **orange-breasted pigeon** and the **grey-fronted pigeon** are both green but have distinguishing features for which they are named. The **Bengal green pigeon** is a large, clumsy bird, easily identified by its yellow legs; other pigeons have red legs. The low, mournful call of the **emerald dove**, a much smaller and darker bird, is heard frequently. Its flight is extremely rapid and straight, yet somehow the emerald dove manages to avoid vines and tree trunks with remarkable skill. Pairs of pinky-grey-coloured **spotted doves** are probably the most obvious as they search roads and open ground for seeds.

Working up and down tree trunks, woodpeckers search for insects, often picking off pieces of bark with their stout, pointed bills. With 13 species recorded so far in Chitwan, correct identification is often difficult. The **three-toed golden-backed woodpecker**, a brilliant species with red, yellow-orange, black and white colouring, is the most common, although both the similarly coloured large and lesser golden-backed woodpeckers are also seen regularly. The **large golden-backed woodpecker**, a shy bird with a spotted breast and piercing call, is usually seen alone or in pairs. The **lesser golden-backed woodpecker** is much bolder and is often found in small parties in open forests. Another group of frequently seen woodpeckers has more subdued grey and green colouring. Rapid tapping usually indicates the presence of the **grey-crowned pigmy woodpecker**, a petite bird with a black and white laddered back. In contrast, the **small yellow-naped woodpecker** announces its presence with only weak tapping, but has a loud, screeching call. The **small scaly-bellied woodpecker** is partial to acacia trees. Like the **black-naped woodpecker**, it is also seen on the ground searching for ants and beetles. The black-naped species is rather shy, often edging up and down tree trunks on the opposite side to the observer.

Drongos are other common residents of the forests and open country of the Park. Black, with long forked tails, they often sit on exposed points watching for insect prey. The **little bronzed drongo**, the larger **crow-billed drongo**, the **white-bellied drongo** and the **ashy drongo** are all seen regularly in sal and riverine forest. The **black drongo** is very common around cultivated land, but also likes mixed grassland and riverine forest or open sal forest.

Flowering kapok trees are attractive to the **hair-crested drongo**, a heavy bird with upturned corners to its slightly forked tail. Sal forests are the preferred haunt of racquet-tailed drongos. Although seen less frequently, racquet-tailed drongos are easily recognised by their long, wire-like outer tail-feathers which sport racquet-like ends. The **large racquet-tailed drongo** has a distinctive crest which the **small racquet-tailed drongo** lacks.

Unlike the black-headed shrike, which prefers open country, the

The shy spotted dove (above) builds a flimsy twig nest to support its two eggs. (Right) The neat cup-shaped nest of the paradise flycatcher.

Insectivorous woodpeckers (below) and drongos are common in the Park's forests. The black drongo (below right) also likes open country.

wood-shrikes and cuckoo-shrikes are forest dwellers. Most wood-shrikes are a drab brown, but cuckoo-shrikes are grey. All have a distinctive dark eye-stripe and a strong, hooked bill.

Although they belong to the same family as wood-shrikes and cuckoo-shrikes, minivets are much more colourful birds. Both the **scarlet minivet** and the **long-tailed minivet** have red and black males and yellow and black females. While the scarlet minivet is a year-round resident, the long-tailed variety is not as common, visiting the Park in winter only. Less vividly coloured, the **small minivet** is also a resident. The **rosy minivet**, a pale pink and grey bird, may also breed in Chitwan, but this has not been confirmed.

The **paradise flycatcher**, daintiest of all the birds found in Chitwan's forests, is unmistakable with its long tail fluttering ribbon-like as it flies. Mature males are snow white, except for a crested black head. First-year males are similar to females, with short tails, light fawn breasts, cinnamon backs and wings. In their second year, males grow longer tail feathers but still retain the females' colouring. The white feathers come in their third year. Arriving in March from the south, the paradise flycatcher stays throughout summer to breed.

In contrast, the plump, pale brown and grey **Brooks' flycatcher** is unspectacular as it works through low understorey vegetation in sal forests. Brooks' flycatcher is a resident species, as is the **white-throated fantail flycatcher**. The latter, a more conspicuous bird, is often seen swinging from vines and tall grass stalks with its fan-shaped tail flared.

A full, mellow call indicates the presence of a **golden oriole**, a beautiful, bright yellow bird which arrives in March and stays for the summer. The similar **black-headed oriole** is a resident and can be seen all year round, usually in the tops of leafy trees. Females of both species follow the males in markings but are a much duller, streaky yellow.

The sapphire and emerald-coloured pittas arrive in May. These short-tailed birds are seen frequently in summer, searching through leaf litter with their strong bills for insects, worms and other small animals. The **Indian pitta** has a distinctive black eye-stripe and rust-brown breast while the **green-breasted pitta** has bright blue rump and shoulder patches and a rich maroon head.

Cuckoos, notorious for their habit of laying their eggs in the nests of smaller birds, are also summer visitors. The hysterical, ascending call of the **common hawk cuckoo** is often repeated well after dark, earning it the name "brain-fever bird". The **Indian cuckoo** is quieter, with a more musical-phrase-like call, repeated at intervals and quite different from the distinctive "cuckoo" call of the **Eurasian cuckoo**, which it closely resembles. The **drongo cuckoo** has a forked tail like the drongos, but its vent and outer tail-feathers are faintly barred with white. It tends to perch with tail drooping and wings held loosely, uttering a repetitive, rapidly ascending scale of six notes.

Orange-headed ground thrush.

In deep, shaded forests, particularly ravines, two songsters attract attention with their melodic calls. One, the **orange-headed ground thrush**, a conspicuous orange bird with a grey-blue back in males, is often heard during summer, calling a variety of short-spaced phrases. The other is the **shama**, a larger, glossy black member of the thrush family with a chestnut breast, conspicuous white rump and long tail. The shama's long sustained song often fills the jungle air at dusk, throughout the year.

The less tuneful leaf-warblers, small greenish-brown birds which are hard to tell apart, come to the Park in winter. Several species have been recorded, the most common four being the **crowned, large crowned, yellow-eyed** and **dull leaf warblers**. Most warblers place their nests either on the ground, in low bushes, or in balls of moss on branches. In contrast, the **tailor bird** builds its nest between large leaves stitched together with spider webs, often producing two or three broods a year. This small, active member of the warbler family is resident in Chitwan. It is frequently seen, with tail cocked, near the ground, where it is easy prey for predators.

The **white-eye**, a small greenish bird with a bright yellow throat and distinctive white eye-ring, often moves in flocks, the birds following one another through the trees. Although it resembles a warbler, the white-eye does not flick its tail and wings as they do, and belongs to a different family.

Hovering around shrubs, where they probe flowers with their long, curved bills, tiny **scarlet-breasted** and **purple sunbirds** occupy a niche similar to that of the hummingbirds of North and South America. Females of both species are a dull green, but their mates are brilliantly plumaged. Another member of the sunbird family, the **streaked spiderhunter**, often flies restlessly from one treetop to another, or else sits upright on a branch with its head constantly moving.

Heads pointing downward, nuthatches work their way down tree trunks as they search the bark for insects with their long, pointed bills. These thickset birds, with short legs and tails, are year-round residents. The **velvet-fronted nuthatch** is quite conspicuous with its blue back, pinky-grey underparts and bright red bill. It works through the middle of trees and along large branches; the similar, but darker and less brightly coloured **chestnut-bellied nuthatch** hunts in the upper branches.

The tail-cocking, male **robin dayal**, a black and white bird very common in Chitwan during summer, should not be confused with the **black-backed forktail** or any of the pied wagtails. Found mainly along streams in sal forest, the forktail is a much larger bird with a long, forked tail. The two species of pied wagtails are found along rivers and riverbanks.

Birds of Aquatic Habitats

Within the river systems of Chitwan, minor habitats range from damp gravel or sandy islands, still backwaters, fast-moving clear water, and dry boulder banks to grassy or swampy streamsides. Many of the birds frequenting these places visit only during winter, arriving in October and departing again about April. Migratory waterfowl are also only seen when they pass over Nepal in spring and autumn. February seems to be the best month to see many of them.

The wagtails are typical of migratory birds. In summer most wagtail species fly in large, loose flocks to the higher, arid trans-Himalayan regions to breed; winter is spent in warmer southern regions such as Chitwan. Along riverbanks the pied wagtails are the most common species. The **small pied wagtail** comes in many variations of black, white and grey, depending on the subspecies, but all are recognisable by their rapid tail pumping. The **large pied wagtail** differs by being a resident species. The yellow, grey, and yellow-headed wagtails are also fairly common winter visitors and each species is found in a slightly different habitat. The **grey wagtail** prefers stony forest streams and rocky riverbeds. Both **yellow wagtails** and **yellow-headed wagtails** are more likely to be found in wet fields or near shallow, grassy-banked streams.

Waders are numerous along the banks of streams and rivers throughout winter. **Greenshanks, Temminck's stint**, and both **common sandpipers** and **green sandpipers** are frequently seen standing in their typical one-legged pose. All have greyish-brown backs and pale underparts, but the greenshank can be distinguished from the others by its larger size and slightly upturned bill.

Both red-wattled and spur-winged lapwings are also very common resident birds. Although similar in colour, they behave quite differently.

Pairs of ruddy shelduck (above) rest on the Park's rivers during their migratory flight north in winter. The merganser (top right) also flies north for the summer to breed in Ladakh. Two winter visitors, the greenshank and common sandpiper (opposite) share a stretch of riverbank, a favourite haunt of the resident red-wattled lapwing (below right) and the large pied wagtail (below).

121

The noisy, **red-wattled lapwing** usually runs along the ground before taking off, calling stridently in short, repeated staccato bursts as it circles overhead. The **spur-winged lapwing** only voices a much milder "pip-pip-pip" as it flies low over water. It walks with a bobbing movement, and often assumes a hunched position with its head drawn in.

Another wader, the **little ring plover**, likes the edges of sandy islands or mudbanks and is often seen in pairs or family groups, running in fast sprints. A distinct black upper chest-band distinguishes it from other waders. Although resident throughout the year, its numbers increase during winter with the arrival of a migratory subspecies.

Reminiscent of swallows, flocks of **small pratincoles** fly back and forth over stony riverbeds during the morning and evening, catching insects. Throughout the rest of the day they sit amongst the pebbles, facing into the wind with their wings held close. These greyish birds with pointed, black primary wing-feathers and black-tipped white tails are residents.

The **Eurasian thick knee** and **great thick knee** (or **stone plovers**) are two other resident birds found along stony riverbanks. The Eurasian thick knee is conspicuously streaked, whereas the great thick knee, a larger bird, is plainer but has a distinctive black face pattern. Both birds are good runners and strong fliers, but the latter tends to crouch amongst stones when approached.

Completely camouflaged by its pale sandy colouring, particularly when motionless, the **sand lark** is most at home on sandy riverbanks. The darker coloured **bush lark** is found in similar territory, although it prefers slightly grassier areas. It is identified from its relative by a rufous wing patch. Both birds are weak fliers; either crouching to avoid being seen or else running along the ground rather than flying when approached.

More often associated with the sea, gulls and terns are fairly common on Chitwan's rivers. Both the **black-headed** and **great black-headed gulls** are winter visitors here. The great black-headed gull is identified by its large size and massive yellow bill. The **Indian river tern** and **black-bellied tern** are resident birds. They have similar colouring, but the former has a swallow-like tail and a yellow bill. In spite of its name, the smaller, black-bellied tern sometimes sports a white belly in winter. Small groups of black-bellied terns often gather together on sandbars for the night, or are seen skimming low over the water, flying with their bills turned down.

The orange-tan coloured **ruddy shelduck** is also very common during winter, with large groups resting or feeding on all the Park rivers. Extremely strong fliers, they migrate across the Himalaya in large groups, sometimes resting on lakes as high as 4700 m. The **merganser**, a duck common on the Rapti and Narayani rivers from October to April, tends to stay in the water rather than rest on the edges. The sexes of this duck usually form separate groups and also look entirely different. Males are mainly white with black heads, while females are brownish with deep tan heads and necks.

Large groups of **pintail ducks** visit in February and March. Other, less commonly seen migratory ducks are **mallards, gadwalls, wigeons, shovelers** and **pochards**.

Tall and stately, the storks are unmistakable. The **open-billed stork**, a greyish-white bird with black wings and tail, is often seen standing motionless in ponds, searching for snails, which it will slit open with its specialised bill. Large groups of open-billed storks often gather in trees at the edges of lakes. **White-necked storks** also haunt the edges of marshes and lakes. During winter, **black storks** are common along open riverbeds. The **black-necked stork**, another winter visitor, is seen less frequently. Tall and heavily built, the **lesser adjutant stork** is a strange-looking bird with a naked head and large bill. It prefers grassland swamps or canals and damp fields adjoining the Park. **Painted storks** are also seen occasionally during summer along the banks of the Narayani River.

Although often associating with storks, the **black ibis** is easily distinguished by its smaller size and long, conspicuously decurved bill. The best identification marks for the black ibis are a white shoulder patch which shows as it takes flight, to describe slow, wide circles before alighting again.

Large cormorants gather on riverbanks in winter. In summer they move northward along rivers towards the mountains.

Along river shallows and lakes, egrets and herons search for small fish, tadpoles and frogs. **Cattle egrets** and **little egrets** are of equal size, but the cattle egret has some tan colouring during the breeding season. Usually solitary and shy, the **large egret** has a longer neck and head than the **intermediate egret**, which is often found in small, scattered flocks. Both purple and grey herons are large birds which might be confused with storks, except that in flight a heron's neck is drawn back in an "S" curve and not stretched out straight. They are mainly winter visitors. The dark-coloured **purple heron** is usually found in marshy areas and ponds, whereas the **grey heron** prefers large rivers and lakes. In flight, the white wings of the **pond heron**, a very common bird, distinguish it from the **little green heron** and the **night heron**. Little green herons like banks overlooking rivers and ponds; night herons are often seen in groups, sitting motionless in tall trees or reeds at the edges of lakes.

The **darter**, another resident of Chitwan's ponds and lakes, often sits on stumps with its wings outstretched, or else swims with only its long, snake-like head showing above water. Cormorants are winter visitors. They look similar to the darter, but lack its silvery streaking and very long neck. They swim with their bills pointing upward. The **large cormorant** has white on its throat and often congregates in large groups on rivers. The **small cormorant** is less common and is usually solitary or sometimes seen in small groups.

In marshes and along the edges of grassy ponds and streams, the **brown crake** searches for food, its cocked tail constantly flicking. The **Indian gallinule**, a winter visitor, is recognised by white on its vent, wings and tail. It tends to swim in groups amongst vegetation on the top of water. Accompanying the Indian gallinule are usually one or two **white-breasted waterhens** and groups of **purple gallinules**. The latter are plump, purplish birds with short red bills.

A flash of brilliant blue attracts instant attention as a **white-breasted kingfisher** dives to catch a fish or grasshopper. A maroon back and white breast distinguish this species from the **Eurasian kingfisher**, a smaller species common near rivers and lakes, and the **blue-eared kingfisher**, which prefers shaded forest streams. The **stork-billed kingfisher** is usually seen along open forest streams and near ponds where it waits patiently for fish, lizards and mice to appear, prey easily caught in its large, dull-red bill. In contrast, the **little pied kingfisher** is constantly active, hunting by hovering high above rivers, then plunging straight down.

Darting in and out of nest holes in riverbanks, and flying rapidly overhead, **sand martins** communicate with high-pitched squeaks. Like **barn swallows**, sand martins are resident birds. The **striated swallow**, however, a species common to Asia, Africa and Europe, comes only in the summer. Both barn and striated swallows prefer open country around the edges of the Park.

The lesser adjutant stork (right), black ibis (above) and open-billed storks are seen in and around the Park all year round.

Birds of Prey

Birds of prey constantly soar overhead, particularly near the edges of the Park where poultry and livestock offer an easy source of food. Many are difficult to identify because of similarities in colouration and size. Even within the same species there can be considerable variation and young birds often have different plumage from their parents. A good example of this is the **honey kite**, which often hunts over forests or clumps of trees bordering fields. This raptor varies in colour from dark to almost white in young birds, but can be identified by one to three dark stripes across the tail. At close range it is possible to see the stiff facial feathers which presumably protect the bird from stings when it eats bees and honey.

The **dark kite** is common around the Park boundaries, where it can steal chickens from villages. When breeding, its loud, interrupted, squealing call is often heard during the hot part of the day. The much smaller **shikra**, a sparrow hawk, sometimes perches on vantage points in trees, or is seen flying swiftly between bushes or low trees where it captures small birds.

Sitting bolt upright in forest trees, the **crested serpent eagle** waits for jungle fowl, pheasants or snakes to present themselves for supper. In contrast, the **white-eyed hawk** tends to sit sluggishly, then drops straight to the ground to pick up insects. Its flight is usually low, with rapid wingbeats, followed by a sudden banking upward to a perch.

The dark, brown-coloured **marsh harrier**, a winter visitor, hunts by sailing over streambeds, grasslands and marshes, while the graceful, long-winged **osprey** hovers over large river pools before suddenly

A crested serpent eagle watches for prey from the branches of a simal tree.

The white-backed vulture is a bold scavenger common throughout the Terai.

plummeting into the water. The rough soles of the osprey's feet are an adaptation for holding slippery fish. Although some osprey appear to be resident in the Park all year, their numbers increase during winter months when migratory birds arrive from trans-Himalayan regions.

Vultures and griffons are mainly scavengers, feeding on the decaying flesh of domestic and wild animals. Over forests and open country the most commonly seen are the **Eurasian griffon**, the smaller **Indian griffon**, and the **white-backed vulture**. The Indian griffon and white-backed vulture are resident birds and similar in size; the Eurasian griffon is a winter visitor. The **Egyptian vulture**, a white bird with a yellow head and black flight feathers, is another winter visitor which frequents open country around the Park boundaries.

Nocturnal hunters are represented by four species of nightjars and eleven species of owls. **Nightjars** are strange looking birds with small bodies, flat heads and large mouths. Although rarely seen during the day because of their camouflaging brown colouration, they are frequently heard at night uttering their loud, repeated calls. Flight is irregular and moth-like as they hunt over grassy areas near forest edges or on cultivated land for moths, beetles, and other insects.

Owls are often seen during the day as they rest in forest trees. Smallest is the **scops owl** which appears to have pale, buff-coloured spectacles. **Jungle owlets** and **barred owlets** are slightly bigger and both have barred black, white and brown breasts. When alarmed, the barred owlet swings its tail from side to side; the jungle owlet just squats with its head pulled in. The **brown hawk owl**, a much larger bird, has a pale breast with brown spots. It sits immobile in leafy trees during the day but becomes active at dusk, flying out to catch insects and returning to the same perch each time. Its loud call is frequently heard in the evenings.

House walls are made from the hard stems of grass, then plastered with a mixture of mud and cow dung.

7. People of the Land

The Tharu

In spite of malaria, ethnic groups such as the Bote, Musahar, Kumal and Tharu have lived in the Chitwan area for hundreds of years. It is possible that they have developed immunity to the disease over centuries, but science has yet to prove this. Although the culture and population of the Tharu has been diluted by the dramatic increase in hill peoples settling in the area over the past 30 years, they are still the major ethnic group. The Tharu are considered to be the true residents of Chitwan and it is for this reason that they are described here.

Various theories have been put forward as to where the Tharu came from, but no definite conclusions have been reached and their origins remain obscure. Ethnically they are a Mongoloid people and it is thought that they have gradually spread westwards from northeast India. Dark-skinned and long-limbed, these shy, unobtrusive people lived in gentle harmony with the land. Essentially rice-growers, cattle-breeders and fishermen with a strong cultural identity, they cleared areas of forest for cultivation. Living on the edges, they used the forests for grazing their cattle and for the fruits, vegetables, firewood, timber, animals and other resources it provided.

Small dolls keep a Tharu girl entertained.

Distinct from other ethnic groups, the Tharu still live only in the Inner and Outer Terai of Nepal and northern India, and always near rivers. There are many different groups of Tharu. The group described here are the Tharu living along the borders of the Park, in the Chitwan Valley. While there are similarities between all the groups, each varies in dialect, social practices and customs. Generally their language is similar to north-Indian dialects of Bhojpuri and Awadhi. Even among Chitwan Tharu there are significant differences between those of Nawalparasi District on the western side of the Narayani River and those of Chitwan District to the east.

Socio-economic Organisation

In the past the Tharu rotated their crops, using a plot of land for 2 to 4 years then, allowing it to lie fallow for several more. Many cattle were kept to plough the land and to provide manure. At that time there was no land register as cultivation was not permanent. People had the right to use the land and own the crops. This changed when land registration was implemented in 1950. Many Tharu did not understand the need to register land in their own names and as a result much was lost to other people. Consequently, many are now landless and work for others.

Cattle grazing on fallow land are watched to stop them straying into crops.

Under the old *adhya* system of land tenure, half the crop goes to the tiller and half goes to the landowner. Another system, *theka*, gives a worker a fixed amount of produce or money for each *bighaa* (approximately 0.6 ha) worked. Both systems are common today.

The biggest landowner in a village is often known as the *Jimindar*. During the Rana rule the Jimindar acted as a tax collector for the government and was entitled to a percentage of the revenue collected. This position enabled him to become wealthy and powerful. Former Jimindar families are still important in village communities.

Quiet and non-aggressive, Tharus have at times been labelled as ignorant, primitive, and as having no culture. Preferring to be farmers, they have not sought education and this has led to economic naiveté in the past. Certainly their unassertiveness has caused them to be an unnoticed and underprivileged minority; yet behind these gentle people lies a strong cultural tradition.

Religion

Tharu society centres around agriculture, and their religion, which is strongly influenced by Hinduism. Religious organisation occurs on three levels — district, village and family — with each level having its own priest.

The *Rajgurau*, or district priest, holds a special, hereditary position, presumed to be linked to the old hill kingdoms. At that time priests were given a royal seal which permitted them to practise certain rituals. In Nawalparasi District an important ritual is performed by the Rajgurau every 3 years, to protect the whole area from many things. It takes place at three different shrines over a 5-to-6-day period and is attended by all village priests. During the ceremonies the priests attain a trancelike state, and many goats, chickens and pigeons are sacrificed. This ritual has not been performed in Chitwan recently as many traditions have been lost or discontinued, because of outside influences.

In the centre of most villages is a shrine, usually a small platform on the ground near a tree. Gods of the shrine are usually represented by stones, or pieces of wood. The main god, which all shrines are named after, is *Brahmaawaa*, who is supposed to eat goats and pigeons. Lesser gods are *Parihar*, who likes pigs, and *Thanagaidi*, who symbolises danger in the jungle and is linked with protection from wild animals. Others are *Jakhin*, who prefers chickens and is linked with good harvests; *Dihacandi*, a goddess; and *Jogi Haawaa*, a god who will cause destruction if not worshipped regularly.

The village priest, *Gaongurau*, performs rituals involving his community. Called *badhna*, these rituals are held on fixed dates. No work involving the use of ox-carts is done during badhna. In Sauraha

An elaborate and unusual shrine in the corner of a private garden.

this tradition has almost disappeared because of tourism and outside influences. During the *asari badhna* in June–July, small sticks are hammered into the ground to destroy bad spirits and to appease the god Thanagaidi. Although still performed annually in Nawalparasi, the asari badhna no longer takes place as often in Chitwan.

Another badhna is held in October–November to protect the new rice crop from insects. When ready for harvesting, the first cuttings of rice are offered to the gods at the village shrine.

Occasionally, if too many people die from an epidemic or other unusual causes, the community may decide to hold an extra badhna. At this time the whole village is closed to outsiders, and many animals are sacrificed.

Each household also has its own *Ghargurau* who performs rituals when family members become ill. The position of family priest is not hereditary and each is chosen by the family. A Ghargurau's services are rewarded with a fixed amount of grain.

An important family ritual, performed by the Ghargurau in May–June, is to appease the divinities associated with women. Tharus believe that the bad influences generated by the gods of a woman's natal home move with her to her husband's house when she marries, and that these gods can cause sickness.

Family Ties and Rites of Passage

Although there is no true clan system, Tharus are vaguely divided into sub-groups, members of which can intermarry. The common family names of Mahato, Chowdhari, and Mukhya used today are derived from various prestigious titles bestowed by the Ranas in earlier times.

Families used to be very large and all members lived under one roof. This provided manpower for farming. Nowadays families tend to split up because of changing economic conditions and smaller land units. Family members still work together, with each having some responsibility. Young children are rarely ill-treated, and family members are always polite to one another.

Marriage is usually between people of the same district or main group. For example, Chitwan and Nawalparasi Tharus will intermarry, but they will not marry Tharus from the Dang-Deokhuri District to the west or the Parsa District to the east. The most auspicious months for weddings are Phagun (mid February to mid March) and Baisakh (mid April to mid May), although they can be held at a few other times. During weddings there is much feasting and dancing if the families can afford it.

Previously, Tharus were married at any age, often when very young. Occasionally even unborn children were "married", but if both turned out to be of the same sex, the marriage was annulled. New laws on the minimum age for marriage have now made this practice illegal.

Most Nawalparasi Tharu marriages are arranged and follow the traditional Hindu custom of giving a virgin girl. Unlike many Hindu societies, however, Tharus have high regard for their daughters and there is no expensive dowry. The girl's family must give a blanket and a pillow and the boy's father may give jewellery and a sari. Traditionally, wedding rituals were performed by a family elder but are now often done by a Brahmin priest.

Chitwan Tharus are not as strict as other groups in their choice of partners, and marriage can take place between anyone except close relatives. Marriage by choice is common. Sister exchange, when a sister of the groom marries a brother or close relative of the bride, is still practised by some Chitwan families. Chitwan Tharus also have ritual friendships which link families. Members of these families cannot marry as they are considered to be related.

Unlike orthodox Hindus, Tharus can divorce and remarry. Occasionally a man will take more than one wife. Polyandry is not recognised or practised, but levirate, where a man marries his elder brother's widow, does take place so that children remain in the man's family.

After childbirth, women are confined to their house, always next to a fire for warmth, for up to 10 days until the baby's umbilical cord falls off. The child is named any time after this, but without any special ceremony. Both mother and baby are considered polluted until after a purification ceremony when they bathe and special purifying water is sprinkled over them.

When a death occurs in a family, the sons or relatives nearest to the deceased observe strict mourning for 13 days afterwards. During this time they must show their mourning by carrying a stick with a white cloth attached. Bodies are either buried or cremated, depending on the family's wishes or tradition, their wealth or the availability of wood, or on ritual prescriptions in the case of unnatural death. Burial or cremation of adults and older children always takes place near the edge of a river, but toddlers and babies are buried in earthenware pots under a nearby road, without any ceremony.

Villages and Houses

The usual village pattern is of several houses grouped together, around an open area, with a communal well or water pump. Originally most households were related, but today villages often contain people from other ethnic groups. The houses of these other people are usually painted on the lower half with an orange-red wash.

Rectangular in shape, Tharu houses are always oriented north-south. They are made from the stems of tall grasses plastered over with a mixture of pale grey mud and cow dung. Very small windows, often no more than narrow slits, allow a little light in and help to keep the interior cool. Roofs are thatched or else covered with small, rounded tiles.

Traditionally, houses were very large and single-storeyed but nowadays they tend to be smaller and higher, often with an upper floor for sleeping or storage. Upper-storey walls are usually left unplastered to allow better circulation of air. Where there is no upper floor, rafters are used to store farming implements, baskets and grass fibre for making ropes and mats. Clothing is occasionally stored in big, lidded baskets which are hung in nets from the roof or rafters.

The kitchen is located in a separate room, usually at the north end of the house, and smoke from the fire helps to keep insects away. There is often another room for eating, but this depends on the size of the house, as does the number of bedrooms. Even the smallest houses usually have a veranda on the eastern side. The *dhiki*, a device for pounding rice to separate the grain from the husk, is housed in a room or building outside.

Older houses have a place in the northeast corner for the family god, usually represented by a small mound of clay or a straw broom. Grain is stored in rectangular bins made from tall grass stalks plastered over

Tharu houses and the communal well at Sauraha. The bundles of grass stems will be used to make new house walls.

Tika decorations.

with mud. There is very little furniture and people generally sit on mats or pads plaited from rice straw. Beds are four-legged wooden frames with rope netting. Occasionally there are low, square stools with carved wooden legs. Generally the interiors of houses are kept very tidy, their mud-plastered floors swept meticulously clean.

Around doors and on outside walls there are usually *tika* decorations made by the women. These are either a handprint or a white, curled symbol made with the side of a closed fist. Although they are now considered merely decorative, tika were probably once linked to ancestor worship.

In front of each house is a courtyard, often partially fenced, with a stout post in the centre. Cattle are tied to a beam which is attached to this post, and are driven around in a circle to thresh the dry wheat or mustard by trampling it underfoot. Cattle and pigs are housed in separate buildings outside, and most houses have a dovecote or small nesting-boxes for pigeons.

Clothing and Jewellery

Traditional clothing for women consists of a short white skirt and a white shawl or length of cloth which is tucked into the waist at front and thrown over one shoulder to cover the breasts. A short, dark blue

Dovecote and tile-roofed house.

Traditional clothes and jewellery are still worn by older women.

136

or black bodice, either sleeveless or with short sleeves, is also worn at times. Because of recent influences, younger women now tend to wear saris. Very young girls today wear Western-style short skirts or pants, sometimes with a top, as other Nepali girls do. The women's clean, well combed hair is usually tied in a distinctive knot at the back of the head.

Many women have their lower legs and occasionally their arms tattooed, often with peacock designs. Mainly for decoration, these tattoos are usually done before marriage by visiting Muslim women, although tattooing can also be done by some Tharu women.

Jewellery traditionally consisted of *tharya*, heavy bracelets worn above the elbows on both arms, and a horseshoe-like neckband called a *hansuli*. Made of silver or an alloy, tharya and hansuli are not often seen nowadays. Decorative silver rings are also worn in noses and ears.

Men's clothing used to be a simple white loincloth and shawl, plus a brimless white cap. Older men still wear these, often with a shirt, but younger men wear Western style clothing. Feet are usually bare, but in the wet summer months wooden shoes with a raised sole and rope thongs for the toes are used for better grip in muddy conditions.

Art and Craft

Besides displaying tika patterns, house walls and the sides of grain storage bins are often decorated with pictures. Traditionally these depict fish, animals and people, but nowadays they also feature buses and aeroplanes. Carts and wheels are decorated occasionally with the closed fist pattern. Originally only yellow and black colours obtained from minerals were used, but others can now be purchased.

Colourful baskets woven from grasses have a multitude of uses.

137

The Tharu were once completely self-sufficient, making everything they needed from natural products around them. Exceptions to this were weights for fishing nets, knives and other metal objects. Ropes and cords are still made from grass and plant fibres. The men are excellent wood-carvers, a skill used in making all their household and agricultural tools, carts and wheels. Many men make superb miniature carts, stools and other toys for their children.

The Tharus' greatest skill lies in their ability to turn local grasses and canes into household items. To combat the heat, fans are made from fine grass stalks, lashed together with different coloured threads in a variety of patterns and edged with a frill of brightly-patterned cotton cloth. These fans are both decorative and practical.

Wide conical baskets called *dauri* are made from the young, inner leaves of *Saccharum spontaneum*. These are coiled, then interwoven and decorated in various patterns with other grasses dyed cerise, green and yellow. Some dauri are decorated lavishly with shells of river crustaceans; others, with pieces of bright-coloured cloth, are made specially for marriage. They are used for holding grains and vegetables, for steaming rice and for storing clothing. The art of making dauri is being lost because the grasses for making them are difficult to find except within the Park, where collection is not permitted.

There are other baskets for holding fish. They can be square or round and usually have narrow necks and an open weave. Water and cooking pots are earthenware. Plates made from the leaves of sal trees and bauhinia vines are still used, particularly during feasts and festivals.

Fishing

Fishing is an integral part of the lives of Tharus and they have developed considerable skills in the art of making nets and fish-traps. Circular casting nets are crocheted from fine thread with a small hooked stick. In the past, even the yarn was made by hand, from a material bought from the Chepang people who dwell in the Mahabharat hills. Now, synthetic thread from the bazaar is used.

Wooden-framed hoop nets are mainly used by women, who catch fish with a scooping movement. Men block the stream and then scoop water and fish into the net, which is raised at one end by two upright sticks.

Fish-traps, made from stiff grass stems and bamboo, are of several different sizes and shapes, depending on where they are to be set. Most are conical in shape. The smallest traps are very long and narrow, for use in drains and irrigation ditches during the monsoon; bigger ones are used in streams and slower water. Large, rectangular traps with several openings are used in rivers.

Skilfully carved toys.

Circular nets and conical traps are used to catch fish.

Food

In the past the Tharu grew only rice, mustard, potatoes and chillis. Herbs, fern shoots and berries from the forest were used as vegetables; fish, chickens, wild birds and animals provided protein. Fledglings were sought after, and the nests of swallows, sand martins and other birds were raided. The Tharu are not hunters of big animals and never used bows and arrows. Birds were caught in noose traps, and small pigs, deer and hares were netted, or cornered and caught by hand. Piglets were often reared for later consumption.

Rice and mustard are still main crops. Due to the influx and influence of hill peoples, maize, wheat, pulses, and a variety of vegetables are now grown as well. On special occasions rice is sometimes soaked and pounded, then made into cakes. Its other major use is to make *jhar*, an alcoholic drink. Before the advent of rice mills, every household dehusked its own rice with a *dhiki*. The rice husks are fed to cattle. Maize cobs are roasted when fresh. Dried corn is ground into meal or popped in hot embers.

Although cows and buffalo are kept, milk and milk products were not used extensively in the past. Even today most milk is sold to people from other ethnic groups. Chickens, ducks, goats and pigs are kept and eaten by most households. Roasted baby pigeons, reared in household dovecots, are considered a delicacy. Aquatic snails collected from ditches, ponds or irrigation canals are also cooked to make a special dish eaten with rice.

Festivals and Dances

The main festival for the Tharus is *Phaguwa* or *Holi*, which takes place during the Nepali month of Phagun (mid February to mid March). The first day of Phaguwa starts on the eighth day of the new moon, and the first 6 days are celebrated with dancing at night by men. Accompanied by flat, one-sided drums, they dance anticlockwise around a group of male singers, visiting each house in turn. No special costumes are used. On the seventh day, the women prepare a special liquor for the next day's feasting. On the eighth day, when the moon is full, people fish and make a deep-fried bread. That night there is more drinking and dancing, again with drums, and a special ceremony involving the burning of a straw hut is performed. The following day, people throw red powder and rub it on each other's faces and many take ritual baths in the rivers. There is more feasting, dancing and worshipping of gods and the festival finally ends with another evening of drum dancing.

Chitwan men also perform stick dances during Phaguwa, accompanied by a flat, one-sided drum. The stick dances performed as

Mustard, an important winter crop, washes the Terai fields in brilliant yellow during December.

During the Maghi festival in mid January, crowds gather at Devghat and bathe in the rivers for purification.

part of the cultural programmes at some Sauraha hotels are based on these Phaguawa celebrations.

The other main festival, *Maghi*, commences on the first day of the Nepali month of Magh (about mid January), with dancing and feasting over 3 or 4 days. During this time the people travel to Devghat, located north of Narayanghat at the confluence of the Kali Gandaki and Narayani rivers, to bathe in the waters for ritual purification.

Women's dances, *jhamta*, are performed during Maghi and also from August to October, when the participants form big circles and sing in high-pitched voices throughout the night. They also have their own ritual festivals, called *jitya*. During *Tij*, a jitya held around the 8 days of the moon of mid August to mid September, women fast for 8 days, then end their fast by eating beaten rice and fruit. In Nawalparasi the men also fast for 1 day, a few days after the women.

Nawalparasi Tharus have three other dances. In the *rasdari* dance, two men, one of them dressed like a woman, dance together accompanied by two tubular, double-ended drums. The *deshi* dance is similar, but only one drum is used. During these dances, which are performed at weddings and on many other occasions, it is traditional to sing love songs and for the dancers to ask for money. Usually the only other musical instruments ever used are small castanets. The third dance, *merari*, is performed indoors and no money is requested from the audience. Fourteen or fifteen drums are used to produce a trance-like state and the dance becomes a ritual for the gods.

The *Sohari* or *Tihar* festival, during the fortnight of the new moon of Ashwin (mid September to mid October), is a time to worship the family gods. Women decorate their homes and make tika decorations around the doors. Nawalparasi girls worship their brothers on the last day of Tihar, following the ancient Hindu custom.

Daily Life

As farmers, the lives of Tharus are organised around the seasons and the planting and harvesting of crops. Summer crops of rice and maize are ready for harvesting from mid September until mid November. They are replaced during the winter and spring by wheat and mustard, both important commercial crops. The wheat is harvested from March through to May.

During December, mustard fields present a spectacular sight with expanses of bright yellow blooms forming a foreground to the clear white mountains. The yellow flowers soon fade and the crop is harvested by the end of January. The seeds are pressed to extract their precious oil, which is used in cooking, and the solid waste is ground up and fed to livestock. Other cool-season crops are lentils and potatoes.

Cattle are important for ploughing the land and providing manure.

A Tharu's life is busy, always occupied with preparing fields for planting, or weeding, harvesting and threshing crops. Men usually do the ploughing, using buffalo and cattle, although women also help to prepare the ground by breaking up clods of ploughed soil. Most weeding is done by the women, but harvesting and threshing are jobs shared by all members of a household. De-husking rice and grinding wheat and maize are women's jobs. Rice mills have relieved women of the de-husking task to a large extent.

Firewood collection is shared by most members of a household, but mixing the mud and dung and plastering houses are jobs done by women, as is food preparation. Water is collected by women from the village well or pump, and is usually carried in a round earthenware pot balanced on the head by a small ring of woven grass. Women also carry other loads this way, but men carry with the help of a yoke. This distinguishes Tharus from hill people, who always carry loads in a basket supported by a headband.

Children also have their allotted tasks, usually helping to collect firewood or watching goats and cattle. Old people who cannot work in the fields look after youngsters or graze cattle, often usefully whiling away the time by making fishing nets.

Medicinal and other plants used by the Tharu

Medicinal plants

ban piyaju (*Crinum amoenum*, Amaryllidaceae): for swollen testicles. An onion the same size as the swollen testicle is dried over a fire of dung briquettes and pine needles (*Pinus roxburghii*). It is then hung in the house and shown to the patient once a day. It is believed that as the onion shrinks, the testicle will get correspondingly smaller.

bathuwa (*Chenopodium album*, Chenopodiaceae): this plant is cooked like a vegetable and eaten to cleanse the stomach, strengthen the body and prevent constipation. Cooked juice from the roots cleanses the bronchial tubes and lungs after excessive smoking of marijuana and tobacco. The leaves are rubbed on the skin to remove nicotine stains.

chatiwan (*Alstonia scholaris*, Apocynaceae): for back pain, high fever and excessive thirst. A jug of water is brought to the tree and a piece of the bark placed in it. The water is kept at the tree and after some time the bark is removed and the liquid drunk.

dharmaruwa (*Rauvolfia serpentina*, Apocynaceae): to protect against snakes. Flowers are hung around the neck, or plants are set in the garden on a cloudy Sunday or Tuesday.

dudkaraya (*Holarrhena pubescens*, Apocynaceae): for stomach and joint pains. The bark is dried and pulverised, then added to water and drunk.

gerguj (*Caesulia axillaris*, Compositae): to stop bleeding. The juice is applied to wounds.

ghorsawa (*Achyranthes aspera*, Amaranthaceae): paste from the roots is mixed with water and massaged into the body for fever associated with illness or hard work. Ash from burnt bark is used on the skin for itchiness.

jamu (*Syzygium cumini*, Myrtaceae): for diarrhoea and stomach pain. The fruit, dried pulverised seeds, paste from the bark, or liquid from the bark cooked in water, are taken.

jinawa (*Shorea robusta*, Dipterocarpaceae): the resin stimulates the appetite and is good for digestion. It is also used as incense during religious festivals.

kannijhani (*Flemingia strobilifera*, Leguminosae): to soothe crying babies. Priests carry out a ritual for babies who cry a lot, placing a twig under the infant's cradle or bedclothes.

khotha (*Asparagus racemosus*, Liliaceae): to aid lactation. A paste from the roots gives strength to breast-feeding women and also stimulates milk secretion in lactating domestic animals. A twig is also hung in the stable of sick animals. The tender shoots are used as a vegetable.

kothaiya (*Ficus hispida*, Moraceae): for earache. A funnel or cone is rolled from a leaf and held together with a thorn. Some embers are placed inside the cone and the liquid which forms is dripped into the infected ear.

larkaiya (*Costus speciosus*, Zingiberaceae): steam from boiling plants is used for swollen feet. A paste made from the inside pith of the stem is applied to wounds to aid healing. Tender stems are used as a vegetable.

patuha (*Helicteres isora*, Sterculiaceae): for infestations of worms in humans and animals. A paste made from the roots is mixed with water and drunk. Only a small dose is taken, as it can be poisonous. This is an effective remedy for humans and animals. Large amounts of tender leaves are also fed to animals. The bark, rotted in water, is used for ropes, and peeled sticks are used as torches or for making fish-traps.

simar (*Bombax ceiba*, Bombacaceae): the resin is taken for worms and diarrhoea with blood. The bark is applied to wounds. Canoes are sometimes made from the wood as it is light. The sticky resin is used to catch birds.

simarlati (*Schefflera venulosa*, Araliaceae): for irregular menstruation with fever. A twig is cut from a tree by a man who must hold his breath while doing it. The twig is then held between the big and second toe of the left foot until the man has removed some of the leaves. At home, in a place cleaned with cowdung, these leaves are ground on a stone with 2½ black peppercorns and water. The liquid is then drunk.

Plants for general use

baniya bans (*Dendrocalamus hamiltonii*, Gramineae). Bamboo used for house construction, basket-making, oil containers, fish-traps, hats and yokes. The tender young shoots are eaten.

ban pharyaruwa (*Dioscorea bulbifera*, Dioscoreaceae). The tuber is used as a vegetable, often fried like a potato, or else pickled.

baruwa (*Saccharum munja*, Gramineae). Canes are used for house walls and fences; the leaves are used for thatch and baskets.

bihid (*Solanum torvum*, Solanaceae). Fruits are used as a vegetable.

citi (*Curcuma aromatica*, Zingiberaceae). The flowers are used as a vegetable.

dabhi (*Imperata cylindrica*, Gramineae). A grass used for thatching, making brooms and ropes.

haria bairi (*Zizyphus incurva*, Rhamnaceae). Fruits, either raw or boiled, are pulped and used like daal, or are pounded with salt and sugar and used as a pickle.

jhaksi (*Saccharum spontaneum*, Gramineae). Canes are used for house construction, the leaves for thatch, and for baskets (with baruwa).

karari (*Saccharum bengalensis*, Gramineae). Canes are used for house construction, fences and fish-traps. The leaves are used for thatch.

katai-k sag (*Amaranthus spinosus*, Amaranthaceae). Tender leaves are used as a vegetable.

khacurati (*Phoenix acaulis*, Palmae). Leaves are used for mats. Fruits and roots are eaten raw, or boiled as a vegetable.

khajuri (*Phoenix humilis*, Palmae). Leaves are used for mats.

kocaiya (*Diplazium esculentum*, Aspicaceae). Young fronds of this fern are eaten as a vegetable.

mahai (*Spatholobus parviflorus*, Leguminosae). An edible oil is obtained from the seeds.

mothi (*Cyperus rotundus*, Cyperaceae). Used to make mats. The tuberous rhizomes can also be eaten.

parra (*Tricosanthes dioica*, Cucurbitaceae). Fruits and tender leaves are used as a vegetable.

sikiyarha (*Vetiveria zyzanoides*, Gramineae). Grass used for fans, small fish-traps, baskets and hats.

yarari (*Acacia pennata*, Leguminosae). Tender leaves are used as a vegetable.

The following have edible fruit:

khurhuri (*Ficus semicordata*, Moraceae).

koilar (*Ficus auriculata*, Moraceae).

kosamha (*Schleichera oleosa*, Sapindaceae).

musleri (*Morus macroura*, Moraceae).

pharsa (*Grewia subinaequalis*, Tiliaceae).

Glossary of Tharu words

anandi. A special red rice, uncooked.

badhna. A village ritual. (Means "to tie" or ritually encircle a certain territory against epidemics or evil forces.)

barahm-taan. Village shrine.

bhanji-yara. Room for eating in.

bhansa. Kitchen.

bhyaawa (Nawalparasi) or **bariyar** (Chitwan). Long, narrow conical fish-traps used in drains and ditches.

byana. A fan.

chicar. Steamed red rice.

damphu. A one-sided drum.

dauri. Wide, conical baskets made from grass.

deli. Square basket for holding fish.

dharya. Largest-sized conical fish-traps.

dhewari. Rectangular fish-traps.

dhiki. Device for de-husking rice.

dhiksari. Room where the dhiki is kept.

gaongurau. Village priest.

ghanka. Scoop or hoop net.

ghargurau. Household priest.

ghatya. White shawl.
gogaili. Medium-sized conical fish-traps.
golauta. Sister exchange.
gunya. Short white skirt worn by women.
hansuli. Silver horseshoe-shaped neckband.
jhamta. Women's dances.
jhumara. Love songs.
jitya. Women's rituals.
kharai. Stems of tall grasses.
khok. Room for sleeping in.
khoki. Fishing net.
kulderata. Household or family god.
lahenga. Special coloured skirt worn by men when dancing.
mandal. A double-ended drum.
munja. Young narrow leaves of *Saccharum spontaneum*.
osara. Veranda.
paini. A bottomless basket for steaming red rice.
patahi. Rectangular grain storage bin.
perugo. Round basket for holding fish.
phana. Net for catching animals.
rajgurau. A district priest.
sanghawa. Ritual friends.
siro. Thatch grass (*Imperata cylindrica*).
tharya. Silver bracelets worn above the elbows.
tika. Decorations made with the hand around doors and on walls.

The annual grass-cutting season gives people access to an important resource which is no longer available outside the Park.

8. From the Other Side of the Fence

The Royal Chitwan National Park has been an undoubted success in terms of preserving several endangered species and their habitat. This success, however, has been at a price, and has generated an increasing number of conflicts between local people and Park management.

A Day-to-day Struggle

As a result of strict habitat protection, rhinoceros, deer, wild pig and tiger numbers have increased dramatically — to the extent that they are now regarded as a nuisance by people living on the periphery of the Park. When life is difficult, and food produced is not enough to feed all the members of their families, it is small wonder that Chitwan farmers cannot understand why the forest is being kept solely for wildlife that destroys crops.

Before the Park was established, local people were able to collect as much firewood, thatch grass, herbs and cattle fodder as they needed. Now they are forced to burn stubble and dung for fuel, and cattle are often undernourished through a lack of good grazing. The dung burnt on fires should be used on fields as fertiliser, but now farmers must buy chemical fertiliser, which is expensive and in many cases unaffordable. Grass for thatching house roofs can only be collected during 2 weeks of the year and not at any other time. Except on public rights of way, an entrance fee is levied even to enter the forests, which were once free for all to use.

When faced with a day-to-day struggle for survival it is little wonder that the average Chitwan farmer knows little about conservation, nor has any interest in its relevance to him. Convincing people that preservation of forests and wildlife is in their long-term interests is one of the main challenges faced by Park managers.

Too Many People

Continued increases in human population (2.6 per cent per annum) in the area surrounding the Park mean that every day more forest is used for fuel and fodder or cleared for people to dwell on and to grow food. New settlers, many of them illegal, continue to come to the Terai, often bringing their cattle with them. Emaciated and sickly, these animals add to the already severe problem of overgrazing, and their diseases could spread to wild animals. With more and more people depleting the

Inadequate grazing for huge numbers of domestic cattle tempts farmers to let their stock wander into the Park.

resources of the dwindling forests outside the Park, illegal firewood collection and grazing within the Park show a parallel increase.

In the early 1970s it was estimated that more than 20,000 domesticated stock used the Park for grazing. This large number was maintained by the availability of food in the forest, but only at the expense of the wildlife. Since restrictions on grazing have been imposed, the number of domesticated cattle has fallen, but illegal grazing along the fringes of the Park is still a problem.

With the continued destruction of forests bordering Chitwan, the Park is becoming more and more an island in a sea of humanity. The increase in agricultural land use everywhere is now threatening the Park. With little forest left to soften the impact of monsoon downpours, the amount of silt being washed into the rivers has increased dramatically, altering the aquatic ecosystem. During peak floods nowadays, rivers frequently change course and inundate areas of previously high ground. Where grazing has been controlled, such as on riverbanks within the Park, thick, matted grasses effectively trap sand and silt and help to control erosion. On steep banks the reverse occurs. The river cuts into the bank and erosion is severe. This is particularly noticeable on the north bank of the Rapti River, where several hectares of agricultural land have fallen into the swirling monsoon floodwaters each summer. As far as the local people are concerned, floods and landslides are generally believed to be acts of the gods and therefore uncontrollable. Unless erosion of banks is controlled, there is little hope for halting the annual destructon.

Crop Damage

Crop destruction by wild animals ranges from as low as 10 per cent to as high as 90 per cent in areas around the Park. Rhino, deer and wild boar are attracted by rice, wheat, maize and mustard crops, and are not easily stopped. Fences and ditches have proved to be ineffective. Large flocks of parakeets also cause damage to grain crops just before harvest.

Villagers try to deter marauding animals by keeping watch at night from raised platforms scattered throughout the fields. Although they spend many sleepless nights making noises to frighten away wildlife, the method has only limited success. Chital and pigs are intimidated relatively easily, but the rhino is not so easily discouraged.

Problems with Predators

Predation of livestock by tigers and leopards is also a major problem. It has been estimated that domestic cattle constitute 30 per cent of tiger kills along the edges of the Park. Most cattle killed are those which have wandered into the Park or are being grazed illegally. In cases such as this the owner has no recompense. When the price of a buffalo represents savings from 4 years of hard labour, it is understandable that the owner feels resentment toward the Park.

Animal attacks on humans also cause resentment, even though the number of people killed annually is very small compared to deaths by natural causes. This comparison is small comfort to bereaved families. Tigers are not the only animals which kill humans. Every year three to five people are mauled or trampled to death by rhinos, usually while they are cutting thatch grass. Each incident increases ill-feeling toward the Park and arouses public opinion against it.

Effects of Tourism

The promised benefits of tourism have not materialised and few jobs have been generated in spite of the tourist industry's assurances. Although tourism is a service-oriented industry, only a small number of locals are employed, and then only in menial jobs, mainly because of the shortage of educational opportunities in the area. The well-paid jobs are taken by more highly educated people from outside Chitwan and even from outside Nepal. The Park itself employs a number of local people and is perhaps their biggest employer. As with tourism, these jobs are seasonal and only a small segment of the population derives any benefit.

A rapid increase recently in the number of facilities at Sauraha, aimed at the budget tourist, has provided some direct benefit to an isolated segment of people but little else to increase earnings for the majority. Because of competition, prices charged for services are low, leaving little margin for any profit. Another detrimental effect of tourism is the rapid rate of inflation it has caused locally. The law of supply and demand pushes prices up, particularly when consumption is not matched by a parallel increase in supply. The only people to benefit are a few merchants and traders; the majority of the people lose.

Tourism has also had a direct effect on the Park's ecosystems. In addition to the 400-plus Park staff who live within the Park area, nearly 40 elephants regularly graze and consume 10,000–14,000 kg of vegetation each day. The constant use of elephants has caused many areas to become crisscrossed with their tracks. This is perhaps preferable, though, to the dust, damage and noise from too many vehicles using the Park's few roads.

Grass — an Annual Benefit

As a compromise, the National Park administration allows grass cutting for 2 weeks every winter. Prior to 1978 this was refused. For a nominal fee, each household can harvest as much grass as its members can gather during the season. Motorised vehicles and bullock carts are not permitted, so both rich and poor have equal opportunity to take as much as they require. The purpose of the fee is not to earn revenue for the Park but to maintain records. In 1987 nearly 60,000 people entered the Park during the 2-week grass-cutting season. It has been estimated that each person removed over 1 tonne of grasses, valued in total at nearly 10 million rupees (US$451,836).

Villagers come from as far as 50 km away to harvest grass, as settlement, grazing and agriculture mean the Park is now the only place where it is available. Consequently, people realise that the Park has preserved a valuable resource for them. In the past the tall grasses were constantly grazed, never reaching full enough maturity to be of use to them.

Another benefit to recently emerge from the grass cutting is yet to be evaluated. Since these tall grasses can be used to manufacture paper, selling it to the paper mill at Narayanghat for a profit has replaced the traditional use for which the concession was established. A side benefit of using grass instead of wood for making paper is that it eases the pressure on the forests, already a precious commodity. The illegal collection of firewood during the grass-cutting season has also lessened as people prefer to take grass and earn cash.

The shorter **khar** (*Imperata cylindrica*) used for thatching is usually harvested during the first few days of the cutting season. After this the tall grasses are burned. This removes leaves and dry outer parts, leaving tall canes which are then easily cut, for use in house walls. Other products taken are **sabai grass** (*Eulaliopsis binata*) and the shrub **patuha** (*Helictres isora*) for making ropes. Ropes made of patuha bark are used for tethering animals as they are unpalatable.

The burning is followed by rapid regrowth, which provides nourishing food for the Park's ungulates. Nevertheless, the annual burning raises a few questions. How many small and possibly rare or endangered animals such as the ground owl, hispid hare or tortoises are killed by fire each year? Fire is not entirely a natural phenomenon, but a human activity practised for hundreds of years to maintain the grasslands. Should the practice be continued? It appears that fire maintains the grasslands and without it the nature of the Park would change.

Humans have been present in Chitwan for hundreds of years. There seems little doubt that their activities have had impact on the vegetation and wildlife, yet in the past the number of people was too low to cause serious habitat destruction.

Conservation Efforts

Attempts to meet the basic needs of the local people are being made with schemes for firewood and fodder plantations. Some more enterprising villagers have started agro-forestry and are implementing grazing controls along riverbanks. The resulting growth of dense grasses can be cut and stall-fed to cattle. Stall-feeding a smaller number of healthier and more productive cattle is beneficial to all. Dung from stall-fed cattle can be used to run low-capacity methane plants, which can make a moderate-sized family self-sufficient in fuel.

To reduce firewood consumption, villagers are encouraged to use improved stoves with a greater fuel efficiency than traditional open fires. Producing vegetables and poultry to supply the growing hotel and tourist industry is another scheme being promoted to diversify the local economy and provide extra cash. Many residents of Sauraha are now aware that their future livelihood lies in servicing the tourist trade, and that it is in their own interests to preserve the Park. Other villagers living around the Park would also care more about it if they understood the value of the Park's wildlife to them. Perhaps the most important element, to bring about an awareness of conservation and how it can effectively help local people, is education. Regular meetings between Park staff and local village leaders, to discuss problems, are encouraged.

Nevertheless, people must remember that animals were in Chitwan before humans and have as much right to live as humans do. If the Park were not protected, and people were allowed to continue grazing cattle and freely taking firewood, timber and other products as they did in the past, the forests would soon be depleted. With continued increases in population, it would take little time before there were no forests and grasslands. There would be no resource left — only more hungry people and progressively less productive agricultural land.

It seems clear that the future of Chitwan as a viable natural system, and the well-being of local people, are inextricably linked. Solutions for one can no longer be sought at the expense of the other.

9. A Brief Guide to visiting Chitwan

Where to Stay

Your choice of accommodation when visiting the Royal Chitwan National Park depends entirely on the state of your finances. There are several safari-type operations within the Park which are run under licence from the government. These concessions provide accommodation, either in lodges or tented camps, and a range of activities including elephant rides, jungle walks, jungle drives and boat trips on the rivers, all with accompanying guides. Most of them provide cultural shows or natural history talks in the evenings.

Of these concessions, the oldest established is Tiger Tops Jungle Lodge at the western end of the Park. With years of experience behind it, Tiger Tops offers first-class accommodation and services. Gaida Wildlife Camp, near Sauraha, and the more recently established Chitwan Jungle Lodge and Machan Wildlife Resort at the eastern end offer similar services.

Several other medium-priced lodges at Sauraha also offer good accommodation and jungle safaris into the Park. These are not licensed as Park concessions, so are restricted in their use of elephants and vehicles. There are also numerous budget-type lodges and restaurants at Sauraha, offering low-priced accommodation and food, but little else. At present there is no electricity within the Park or at Sauraha and none of the lodges has air-conditioning or fans. Lighting is by kerosene lamps.

For visitors who find hot weather a problem, the Hotel Narayani Safari at Bharatpur, near Narayanghat, provides modern, air-conditioned accommodation and a swimming pool. This hotel makes a good base for visiting the Park and the surrounding area.

Getting There

If you intend staying at any of the bigger lodges, transport will be arranged for you. Tiger Tops' guests usually fly to Meghauli airfield and are then transported by elephant or Land-Rover to the main lodge, or by boat to the tented camp. Transport to Chitwan Jungle Lodge, Gaida Wildlife Camp and some of the other lodges at Sauraha is usually by car or four-wheel-drive vehicle via the Prithvi Highway, better known as the Pokhara Road from Kathmandu. The scenic 165-km trip, which follows the Trisuli River for part of the way, takes about 5 hours. It is also possible to fly to Bharatpur on the weekly Royal Nepal Airlines flight, but you must pre-arrange transport from the airport or use local buses to get to your accommodation.

Guests of Machan Wildlife Resort are also taken by vehicle, usually via the Tribhuvan Raj Path, the original road from India to Kathmandu. This road crosses the Mahabharat Range at 2500 m, offering splendid views of the Himalaya in clear weather. Alternatively, guests can fly to Simra, and drive to the lodge.

Instead of driving the whole distance to these lodges, many people are now rafting sections of the Trisuli and Narayani rivers. They are met at a pick-up point and transported by road to their accommodation. Most lodges have offices in Kathmandu and can usually offer package programmes that include transportation. Consult them or a travel agent for further information.

For the budget traveller intending to use low-priced accommodation at Sauraha, the usual means of transport from Kathmandu is by bus to Narayanghat and then to Tandi Bazar, about 20 km further east. Buses leave Kathmandu and Narayanghat daily. From Tandi Bazar it is 6 km to Sauraha. There are no buses along this section, so you can either walk it or hire an ox-cart. The pace of an ox-cart is about the same as walking but a ride is often preferable in hot weather and is an enjoyable experience.

If you are travelling to Chitwan directly from India and your point of entry into Nepal is Birgunj, take any bus travelling west via Hetauda and Narayanghat and ask to be let off at Tandi Bazar.

Health Precautions

Although malaria is not common, it is advisable to take some form of antimalarial medication. The usual recommendation is to take chloroquine tablets, starting 2 weeks before going to Chitwan, or anywhere in the Terai, and continuing for 6 weeks after you leave. Check with a doctor before coming to Nepal, or at a medical clinic in Kathmandu.

Mosquitoes and other insects are not usually a problem during winter and the early spring months, but they can be irritating at night from April onwards. They can be kept at bay by burning locally available mosquito coils, and by using a good insect repellent.

If you have been out in the jungle or grasslands, check your body for ticks or mites which you may have picked up. They like warm places such as armpits, ears and crotches. To remove one, apply insect repellent and pull gently. Ensure that you do not leave the insect's mouthparts or head behind as the bite will itch for months and could become infected. Leeches can be removed by applying salt or iodine, or burning with a lighted match or cigarette lighter.

Most of the expensive lodges take care with food preparation and also provide boiled and filtered drinking water for guests. The same should not be expected in the budget hotels at Sauraha. As a precaution against intestinal problems:

• *Never* drink unboiled water. Stick to tea, coffee, beer or reliable brands of bottled drinks. Water can be treated by adding 4 drops of Lugol's solution (2 per cent iodine) to 1 litre of water and waiting 30 minutes. Lugol's solution is available in pharmacies and some cold stores (grocery shops) in Kathmandu. Many chlorine-based water-purifying tablets are ineffective against amoebic cysts and cannot be recommended.

• *Avoid* food that is uncooked. Unless you know that salad vegetables have been treated with iodine, don't eat them. Fruit should be peeled carefully or soaked in an iodine solution (4 drops to 1 litre of water) for 30 minutes before it is eaten.

• *Avoid* food that is not freshly cooked. It can deteriorate quickly in warm weather and may have had flies walking over it.

If you do succumb to an upset stomach, try going without food for 24 hours, but make sure you drink plenty of fluids. Mild upsets are usually self-limiting and gone within 48 hours. Amoebic dysentery and giardia are usually treated with Tiniba 500 (Tinidazole), and bacilliary dysentery with Septrim (sulfa and trimethoprim) or nalidixic acid. These drugs are available at chemists in Kathmandu. Self-diagnosis and treatment are not recommended, however. For serious problems it is better to consult a doctor.

Clothing

For most of the year, particularly during the day, temperatures are warm and only light clothing is needed. Mornings and evenings in winter can be very chilly, requiring a warm sweater or jacket. Early-morning elephant rides can be particularly cold before the sun rises and warms the air enough to dispel the damp morning mist.

Lightweight, loose-fitting trousers and long-sleeved shirts are recommended for elephant riding as they give protection from cuts and scratches while moving through the tall grass and forests. They are also useful at night against mosquitoes.

Boat rides give a different view of the Park and its wildlife.

Canvas shoes or lightweight boots are ideal for walking or elephant riding as they give protection from thorny vines, insects and prickles. Sandals and thongs are suitable only around lodges and villages as they can catch in vegetation and be easily pulled off.

A sunhat or light neck scarf and suncream are often necessary for preventing sunburn. Although it rarely works, the hat or scarf could be useful for throwing down to distract a charging rhino!

Useful Items to take

Binoculars	Umbrella (for sun or rain)
Camera and films	Small first-aid kit containing:
Flashlight	personal medication
Bird identification book	antiseptic ointment
Hat	anti-diarrhoea medicine
Suncream	sticking plaster
Sunglasses	small pair of scissors
Insect repellent	mild analgesics

Visitor Services

Information centres
The Park Headquarters are at Kasara, housed in a Rana hunting lodge. Built in 1939 for the visit of King George VI of England, this lodge was the first building in the Terai to be made of concrete. It now houses a small museum and offices for the Park's warden and staff. The gharial breeding centre at Kasara is open to visitors for a small fee and is well worth visiting.

For many visitors the main entrance and Visitor Centre for the Park is at Sauraha. Displays here give an insight to the Park and its inhabitants. Maps and information leaflets are available at the adjacent Park Entrance Office.

Park entrance fees
All visitors must pay an entrance fee of 65 rupees (approximately US$3.00) to enter the Park. This is likely to increase in the near future. Guests of the concession lodges within the Park pay this fee only once because they are not exiting and entering several times. Other visitors who enter on a daily basis must pay the fee each time they enter. (This can be a potential trap for the budget tourist staying outside the Park.)

Entry permits must be carried at all times, as Park guards often make random checks. People entering the Park without permits can be fined heavily.

Safety

Walking about in the Park is not recommended. If you have to, use a reliable guide who knows his business. The dense, tall grasses prevent any chances of seeing wildlife until you are almost on top of it — a little tricky if you suddenly confront a rhino. Trained guides have certificates to prove they have passed standards set by Park authorities, and visitors should ensure that any guide they use has this certificate. There are several *machans* (viewing towers) in the Park where wildlife can be viewed in safety, and guides can be hired to take you to one. Elephant riding offers the best and safest way to see wildlife, particularly rhinos. The Park is open between 6 a.m. and 6 p.m., and all visitors enter at their own risk.

Elephants

All Park concession lodges have their own elephants for use by their guests. There is a government *hatisar* (elephant camp) at Sauraha and other visitors can usually hire a government elephant to take them into the Park for wildlife viewing. Many people feel that the charge for hiring an elephant is excessive, but it should be realised that the price of a trained one is high and there are additional costs in maintaining the animal in a good working condition. To ensure the elephants are adequately fed, their natural diet of leaves and grass is supplemented daily with about 20 kg of unhusked rice, flavoured with molasses and salt. Fist-sized balls of the rice mixture, either raw or cooked, are carefully wrapped in grass and made into bundles known as *kuchi*. This is a time-consuming business as each elephant eats over 100 kuchi every day.

Three men are needed to take care of one elephant: the *phanit* or driver, who rides on its neck; the *pachhuwa*, who stands behind and often spots game; and the *mahut*, who cleans the stable and attends to other daily chores. The phanit is the most senior of the three and the mahut is the lowest in the hierarchy.

While riding an elephant:

• *Never* call the elephant driver a mahut. This is an insult. The correct term is phanit.

• *Always* hold on tightly when the elephant is preparing to sit or stand. At all times have one hand holding a rope, the saddle or houdah. When the elephant is going downhill, hold the back of the saddle firmly; when it goes uphill hold on to the front. Sometimes an elephant will rumble in its belly. This is because it has smelt a large predator like a tiger and knows it is nearby. On such occasions, hold on tightly.

• *Never*, under any circumstances, grab hold of the phanit. If the elephant has panicked, as it can do if charged suddenly by a rhino or tiger, or is stung by bees, the phanit will have it under control very quickly. By grabbing the phanit you may both fall off together or

prevent him from controlling the elephant.
- *Never* try to jump down from an elephant. The phanit will get the elephant to kneel so that you can get down easily.
- If you drop anything, point it out to the phanit and he will command the elephant to pick it up for you.

Vehicles

Concession lodges have their own four-wheel-drive vehicles for taking guests out on jungle drives. Other lodges operating from outside the Park do not have this right. The use of private vehicles on Park roads is only by permit from the Park authorities at Kasara or Sauraha, or from the Department of National Parks and Wildlife Conservation in Kathmandu.

Boat rides

Visitors staying at concession lodges usually have the option of a boat trip on the Rapti or Narayani river. At Sauraha, dugout canoes (with boatmen) can be hired to take people down the Rapti River, providing an opportunity to see some of the Park's waterbirds. October to November and February to March, when migratory birds are resting in the Park, are particularly good periods. After a boat ride of about an hour, it is usual to walk back to Sauraha while the boatman poles the canoe back upstream. A guide must accompany you on these trips. Fees are set and approved by Park authorities. During summer months, when rivers and streams are swollen by monsoon floods, boat rides can be risky and are not usually undertaken.

Cultural Etiquette

- *Never* swim naked or with very scanty clothing in local rivers unless you are well away from the public eye.
- *Avoid* wearing scanty clothing around villages or when associating with local people. It is considered indecent for women to show the upper parts of their legs.
- *Ask permission* before photographing people. If they indicate that they do not wish to be photographed, don't persist.
- *Don't* give money or sweets to begging children. It only encourages them.
- *Bargaining* over the price of something *beforehand* is an acceptable practice, but once agreed on, don't try to change it afterwards. This applies to food, accommodation and guiding fees as well as goods.
- *Don't* argue with Park staff over the cost of the Park entry fee, an elephant ride or a boat trip. The prices are set by government authorities in Kathmandu and staff are only carrying out their duties.

Appendices

Appendix i

A checklist of fish species collected from rivers bordering the Royal Chitwan National Park

ANGUILLIDAE
Raja bam *Anguilla bengalensis*

BADINAE
Pansierei *Badis badis*

BAGRIDAE
Tengara *Mystus (mystus) vittatus*
Tengna *M. (mystus) cavasius*
Tengri *M. (mystus) osteobragus aor*, *M. (mystus) osteobragus seenghala*

BELONIDAE
Drongahee *Xenetodon cancila*

CENTROPOMIDAE
Chuna *Chanda baculis*, *C. nama*, *C. ranga*

COBITIDAE
Baghee *Botia almorhae*, *B. lohachata*
Chi-chui *Lepidocephalicthys guntea*
Masany guiera *Nemacheilus rupicola* var. *inglisi*
Patai guiera *Nemacheilus botia*

CYPRINIDAE
Asalla *Schizothoraicthys progastus*
Bangel *Labeo angra*
Bitti *Chela laubuca*
Bitti *Danio dangila*, *D. devario*, *D. rerio*
Boralkay *Acrossocheilus hexagonolepsus*
Boudina *Garra gotyla gotyla*
Chipwa *Aspidoparia morar*
Chuna *Osteobrama cotio*
Churee *Oxygaster bacaila*
Daraha *Puntius sarana*
Derwee *Esomus danricus*
Derwee *Rasbora daniconius*
Gollera *Barilius bola*
Goranhi *Chagunius chagunio*
Gurdi *Labeo boga*
Kursar *Labeo gonius*
Laharay *Crossocheilus latius*
Mahingi, mallingi *Semiplotus semiplotus*
Mahseer, sohor *Tor tor*

Motea *Barilius modestus, B. tileo, B. shacra*
Patajuti *Psilorhynchus sucatio*
Pocketa *Barilius bendelisis*
Rohu *Labeo rohita*
Rotar, rotrahee, koran *Tor putitora*
Siben *Amblypharyngodon mola*
Sidra *Puntius chola, P. conchonius, P. sophore, P.ticto, P. titus*
Tair *Labeo pangusia*

GOBIIDAE
Bulbulia *Glossogobius giurus*

MASTACEMBELIDAE
Coochi bam *Mastacembalus armatus*
Melangi bam *M. pancalus*

NANDIDAE
Dokia *Nandus nandus*

NOTOPTERIDAE
Lopsi *Notopterus notopterus*

OPHIOCEPHALIDAE
Casra bhote *Channa punctatus*
Chipli bhote *C. gachua*
Saura *C. marulius*

SCHILBEIDAE
Boysa, boykha, boykhee *Clupisoma garua*
Nemna *Pseudotropius atherinoides*

SILURIDAE
Binhar *Amblyceps mangois*
Borari *Wallago attu*
Borari *Erethistes elongata*
Lundra *Ompok bimaculatus*

SISORIDAE
Cotinga *Glyptothorax cavia, G. hora, G. pectinopterus, G. telchitta,
    G. trilineatus*
Gaunch *Bagarius bagarius*
Teldouray *Pseudecheneis sulcatus*

TETRODONTIDAE
Delpuhi *Tetraodon cutcutia*

Appendix ii

A checklist of plants recorded in the Royal Chitwan National Park

This list is not necessarily complete as new species are continually being added.

Pteridophytes

EQUISETACEAE
Equisetum debile Roxb.

OPHIOGLOSSACEAE
Helminthostachys zeylanicus (L.) Hooker.
Ophioglossum petiolatum Hooker.

SCHIZACEAE
Diplazium esculentum (Retz) SW. ex Schard
Dryopteris sp.
Lygodium flexuosum (Linn) SW.
L. japonicum (Thunb.) SW.
Pteris aspercaulis Wall ex Agardh
P. rittata

SELAGINELLACEAE
Selaginella molliswall

Gymnosperms

GNETACEAE
Gnetum sp.

PINACEAE
Pinus roxburghii Sargent.

Monocotyledons

AMARYLLIDACEAE
Allium cepa L.
A. sativum L.
A. wallichii Kunth.
Crinum amoenum Roxb.

ARACEAE
Gonotanthus pumilus (D. Don) Engler & Krause
Lasia spinosa (L.) Thwaites
Pistia stratiotes L.
Remusatia sp.

COMMELINACEAE
Commelina benghalensis
Commelina sp.
Cyanotis sp.

CYPERACEAE
Cyperus difformis L.
C. digitatus Roxb.
C. mersuri L.
C. niveus Retz.
C. nutans Vahl.
C. pilosus Vahl.

C. rotundus L.
Fimbristylis bisumbelata (Forsk.) Bubani
Kyllingia brevifolia Rottb.
K. colorata (L.) Druce.
Mariscus sumatrensis (Retz.) T. Koy.
M. paniceus (Roetb.) Vahl.
Pycreus globosus (All.) Reiche.
Schoeno-plectus mucronatus (L.) Palla
Scleria laevis Retz.
S. terrestris (L.) Fass.

DIOSCOREACEAE
Dioscorea bulbifera L.

ERIOCAULACEAE
Eriocaulon nepalense Pres ex Bong

GRAMINEAE
Apluda mutica L.
Aristida adscensionis L.
Arundinella nepalensis Trin
Arundo donax L.
Bambusa arundinaceae
B. nutans Wall.
Bothriochloa glabra (Roxb.) A. Camus.
Brachiaria milliformis (Presl.) A. Chase
B. ramosa (L.) Stapf.
Capillipedium assimile (Steudel A. Camus
Centotheca lappacea (L.) Desv.
Chrysopogon aciculatus (Retz). Trin
C. gryllus (L) Trin.
Coix lachryma-jobi L.
Cymbopogon flexuosus (Nees ex Steudel W.)
C. olivieri (Boiss.) Bor.
C. pendulus (Nees ex Steudel W.)
Cynodon dactylon (L.) Pers.
Dactyloctenium aegypticum (L.)
Dendrocalamus hamiltonii Nees & Arn. ex Munro
D. strictus
Desmostachya bipinnata (L.) Stapf.
Digitaria adscendens (H.B.K.) Henr.
D. ciliaris (Retz) Koeler.
D. sectpaviglumae
D. setigera Roth. apud Roem et Schult.
D. violascens Link.
Echinochloa colona (L.) Link.
E. crusgalli (L.) Beauv.
Eleusine indica (L.)) Gaertn.
Eragrostis atrovirens (Desf.) Trin ex Steud.
E. ciliaris (L.) R. Br.
E. coarctata Stapf. apud Hook.

E. japonica (Thunb.) Trin.
E. tenella (L.) P.Beauv ex Roem et Schult.
E. unioloides (Retz.) Nees ex Steud
Erianthus filifolius (Steud.) Hackel.
E. longesetosus Anderss.
E. ravennae (L.) Beauv.
E. rufipilus (Stend) Griseb.
Eulalia fastigiata (Nees) Haines.
Eulaliopsis binata (Retz) C.E. Hubbard
Hemarthria compressa (L.F.) R. Br.
Heteropogon contortus (L.) P. Beauv ex Roem & Schult.
Hygrorhyza aristata (Retz.) Nees ex Wight & Arn.
Imperata cylindrica (L.) P. Beauv.
Leersia hexandra Swartz.
Leptochloa chinensis (L.) Nees.
Narenga porphyrocoma (Hane.) Bor.
Neyraudia reynaudiana (Kunth) Kent et Hitchc.
Osplismenus burmannii (Retz.) P. Beauv.
O. compositus (L.) Beauv
Panicum astrossiaticum
P. cambogiense Balansa
Paspalum distichum L.
P. scrobiculatum L.
Perotis hordeiformis Nees ex Hook. et Arn.
Phragmites karka (Retz.) Trin & Steud.
Pogonatherum crinitum (Thunb.) Kunth.
Polypogon monospeliensis (L.) Desf.
Pseudopogonatherum contortum (Brongy) A. Camus.
Saccharum arundinaceum Retz.
S. munja Roxb.
S. bengalensis
S. spontaneum L.
S. procerum Roxb.
Sacciolepis indica
Setaria glauca (L.) Beauv.
S. pallide-fusca (Schumach.) Stapf & C.E. Hubbard
S. plicata (Lam.) T. Cooke.
Sporobolus diander (Retz.)P. Beauv.
S. fertilis (Stendel) W.D. Clayton
Themeda arundinacea (Roxb.) Ridley
T. caudata (Nees.) A. Camus.
T. villosa (Poir) A. Camus.
Thysanolaena maxima (Roxb.) O.Kuntz.
Vetiveria zyzanoides (L.) Nash.

HYPOXIDACEAE
Curculigo archiodes Gaertn.
Hypoxis aurea Lour.

LEMNACEAE
Lemna perpusilla Torrey.

Spirodela polyrhiza L.
Wolffia globosa (Roxb.) Hartog & Plas.

LILIACEAE
Asparagus racemosus Willd.
Smilax lanceifolia Roxb.
S. ovalifolia (Roxb.) ex D. Don.

MUSACEAE
Musa balbisiana Colla

ORCHIDACEAE
Acampe papillosa (Lindl.) Lindl.
Aerides odorata Lour.
Eulophia explanata
Geodorum pallidum
Ponerorchis sp.
Rhynchostylis retusa (L.) Blume
Vala testacea (Lindl.) Reich
Zeuxine strateumatica (L.) Schlecht.

PALMAE
Calamus tenuis Roxb.
Phoenix acaulis Buch.
P. humilis Royle.

TYPHACEAE
Typha elephantina Roxb.

ZINGIBERACEAE
Costus speciosus (Koenig) Smith
Curcuma aromatica Salisb.
Globba racemosa Smith
Hedychium spicatum Smith in Rees.
Zingiber capitatum Roxb.
Z. officinale Rosc.

Dicotyledons

ACANTHACEAE
Barleria cristata L.
Dicliptera bupleuroides Nees
Echinacanthus attenuatus (Wall. ex Nees) Nees.
Eranthemum purpurascens Nees
Goldfussia nutans Nees
Hygrophila polysperma (Roxb.) T. Anders
H. salicifolia (Vahl) Nees.
Justicia adhatoda L.
J. diffusa Willd.
J. procumbens L. var. Simplex (D.Don) Yamazaki
Lepidagathis incurva Buch.-Ham. ex D. Don
Phlogacanthus thyrsiflorus (Roxb.) Nees

Rungia parviflora (Retz.) Nees
Thunbergia coccinea Wall.ex D. Don.
T. grandiflora Roxb.

AMARANTHACEAE
Achyranthes aspera L.
Alternanthera sessilis (L.) DC
Amaranthus spinosus L.
Deeringia amaranthoides (Lam.) Mer.

ANACARDIACEAE
Buchanania latifolia Roxb.
Lannea coromandelica (Houtt.) Merr.
Mangifera indica L.
Rhus javanica L.
Semecarpus anacardium L. f.

ANONACEAE
Miliusa velutina (Dunal) Hook. f.& Thoms

APOCYNACEAE
Alstonia scholaris (L.) R. Br.
Holarrhena pubescens (Buch-Ham.) Wall ex D. Don
Ichnocarpus frutescens (L.) R. Br.
Rauvolfia serpentina (L.) Benth. ex Kurz
Trachelospermum lucidum (D. Don) K. Schuom.
Vallaris solanaceae (Roth.) O. Kuntze.

ARALIACEAE
Schefflera venulosa (Wight & Arn.) Harris
Trevesia palmata (Roxb.) vis.

ASCLEPIDACEAE
Calotropis gigantea (L.) Dryand.

BETULACEAE
Alnus nepalensis D. Don.

BIGNONIACEAE
Stereospermum chelonoides (L.f.) DC.

BOMBACACEAE
Bombax ceiba L.

BURSERACEAE
Garuga pinnata Roxb.

CANNABACEAE
Cannabis sativa L.

CAPPARIDACEAE
Cleome viscosa L.

CARYOPHYLLACEAE
Polycarpon prostratum (Forssk.) Aschers. & Schweinf. ex Aschers.
Stellaria sp.

CERATOPHYLLACEAE
Ceratophyllum demersum L.

CHENOPODIACEAE
Chenopodium album L.

COMBRETACEAE
Anogneissus latifolius (Roxb. ex DC.) Bedd.
Terminalia alata Heyne ex Roth.
T. bellirica (Gaertn) Roxb. At.
T. chebula Retz.

COMPOSITAE
Adenostemma lavenia (L.) O. Kuntze.
Ageratum conyzoides L.
A. houstonianum Miller.
Artemisia dubia Wall.
Bidens pilosa Linn.
Blumea laciniata DC.
Blumeopsis flava (DC) Gagnep.
Caesulia axillaris Roxb.
Cirsium aevense (L.) Scop
C. wallichii DC.
Crassocephalum crepidiodes (Benth.) S.
Eclipta prostrata Linn.
Erigeron bonariensis L.
Eupatorium adenophorum Spreng.
E. odoratum L.
Gnaphalium luteoalbum
Inula cappa DC.
Launaea aspleniifolia (Willd.) Hook.f.
Saussurea heteromalla (D. Don) Hand-Mazz
Spilanthus nodiflora (L.) Gaertz.
Tridax procumbens L.
Vernonia cinerea (L.) Less.
Xanthium strumarium L.
Youngia japonica (L.) DC.

CONVOLVULACEAE
Argyreia hookeri C.B. Clarke
A. nervosa (Burm.f.) Boy.
A. roxburghii Choisy.
Cuscuta reflexa Roxb.
Ipomoea quamoclit L.
I. pestigridis L.

CORDIACEAE
Cordia grandis Roxb.
Cynoglossum glochidiatum Wall ex Benth.
C. zeylanicum (Vahl) Thunb. ex Lehm.
Ehretia acuminata R. Br.
E. laevis Roxb.

Heliotropium strigosum Willd.
Maharanga bicolor (Wall. ex G. Don) A. DC.

CRUCIFERAE
Raphanus sativus L.
Rorippa nasturtium-aquaticum (L.) Haye K.

CUCURBITACEAE
Cucumis melo L.
C. sativus L.
Diplochylas palmatus (L.) C. Jeffrey.
Edgaria darjeelingensis C.B. Clarke
Herpetospermum pedunculosum (Ser.) Bail.
Lagenaria siceraria (Molina) Standl.
Mukia maderaspatana (L.) Roem.
Solena heterophylla Lour.
Trichosanthes dioica Roxb.
Zehneria indica (Lour.) Keraudren-Aymonin
Z. maysorensis (Wight & Arn) Arn.

DILLENIACEAE
Dillenia indica (L.)
D. pentagyna Roxb.

DIPTEROCARPACEAE
Shorea robusta Gaertn.

ELAEOCARPACEAE
Elaeocarpus tectorius (Louv.) Poir.

EUPHORBIACEAE
Baccaurea ramiflora Lour. Fl Cochinch.
Bischofia javanica Blume.
Bridelia retusa (L.) Spreng.
Croton grandis Roxb.
Drypetes roxburghii (Wall.) Hurusawa.
Euphorbia fusiformis Buch.-Ham ex D.Don
E. hirta L.
Glochidon lancealarium (Roxb.) Voight. H. Subarb.
G. velutinum Wight
Macaranga denticulata (Blume) Muell.-Arg.
M. pustulata King ex Hook. f.
Mallotus nepalensis Muell.Arg.
M. philippinensis (Lam.) Muell.-Arg.
Phyllanthus emblica L.
P. reticulatus Poir.
P. niruri L.
Sapium insigne (Royle) Benth ex Hook.f.
Securinega virosa (Roxb.ex Willd) Baill.
Trewia nudiflora L.

FLACOURTIACEAE
Casearia elliptica Willd.

C. glomerata Roxb.
C. graveolens Dalz.
C. tomentosa Roxb.
Xylosma longifolium Clos.

FUMARIACEAE
Fumaria indica (Haussk.) Pugsley.

GENTIANACEAE
Exacum tetragonum Roxb.
Swertia angustifolia Buch.- Ham ex D.Don

ICACINACEAE
Natsiatum herpeticum Buch.-Ham.

LABIATEAE
Anisochilus pallidus Wall.ex Benth.
Anisomeles indica (L.) Kuntze
Colebrookea oppositifolia Sm.
Eusteralis cruciata (Benth.) Pan.
Hyptis suaveolens (L.) Poit.
Leonurus nepataefolia (Buch.-Ham. ex D. Don) Hara
Leucas cephalotes (Roth.) Spreng.
L. indica (L.) R. Br. ex Vatk.
L. mollissima Wall.
L. plukenetii (Roth.) Spreng.
L. zeylanica (L.) R. Br.
Micromeria integerrium Benth.
Pogostemon benghalensis (Burm. f.) Kuntze
Rabdosia coetsa (Buch.-Ham. ex D.Don) Hara
R. ternifolia (D.Don) Hara
Salvia plebea R. Br.

LAURACEAE
Litsea monopetala (Roxb.) Per.
L. salicifolia (Roxb. ex Nees) J. Hooker
Persea duthiei (King ex Hook. f.) Kos.

LECYTHIDACEAE
Careya herbacea Roxb.

LEGUMINOSAE
Acacia catechu (L.F.) Willdenow
A. lenticularis Buch.-Ham.
A. pennata (L.) Willdenow
A. rugata (Lam.) Voigt
Albizia gamblei Prain
A. lebbek (L.) Benth.
A. odoratissima Benth.
Atylosia scarabaeoides (L.) Benth.
Bauhinia malabarica Roxb.
B. purpurea L.
B. vahlii Wight & Arn.

Butea monosperma (Lam.) Kuntze
Caesalpinia bonduc (L.) Roxb.
C. decapetala (Roth) Alston
Cajanus sativa L.
Cassia fistula L.
C. tora L.
Codaricalyx gyroides (Roxb. ex Link) Hassk
Crotalaria albida Heyne ex Roth
C. pallida Ait.
Dalbergia sissoo Roxb.
D. stipulacea Roxb.
Desmodium microphyllum (Thunb) DC.
D. oojeinense (Roxb.) Ohashi.
D. trifolium (L.) DC.
Erythrina suberosa Roxb.
Flemingia macrophylla (Willd.) Merr.
F. strobilifera (L.) Ait.
Indigofera pulchella Roxb.
Lespedeza eriocarpa DC.
Millettia extensa (Benth) Barker.
Mimosa pudica L.
M. rubicaulis Lam.
Mucuna nigricans (Louv.) Stend.
Phyllodium pulchellum (L.) Desv.
Spatholobus parviflorus (Roxb.) O. Kuntze
Uraria lagopus DC.

LENTIBULARIACEAE
Utricularia aurea Lour.

LINACEAE
Reinwardtia indica Dumort

LOGANIACEAE
Buddleia asiatica Lour.

LORANTHACEAE
Dendrophthoe falcata (L.f.) Etling

LYTHRACEAE
Lagerstroemia parviflora Roxb.
Rotala rotundifolia (Roxb.) Koehne in Eng.
Woodfordia fruticosa (L.) Kurz.

MALVACEAE
Abelmoschus moschatus Medik.
Hibiscus manihot Linn.
H. platanifolius (Willd.) Sweet
Kydia calycina Roxb.
K. jujubefolia Griff.
Sida rhombifolia L.
Thespesia lampas (Cavan.) Dalz et Gibs.
Urena lobata Linn.

MELASTOMACEAE
Melastoma malabathricum L.
Osbeckia nutans Wall.ex C.B. Clarke
O. rostrata D.Don

MELIACEAE
Azadirachta indica A. Juss.
Chisocheton paniculatus L.
Cipadessa baccifera (Roth.) Miq.
Trichilia connaroides (Wight & Arn) Bentv.
Toona ciliata M. Roem

MENISPERMACEAE
Stephania japonica (Thunb.) Miers

MORACEAE
Ficus auriculata Lour.
F. glaberrima Bl.
F. hederaceae Roxb.
F. hispida L.f.
F. racemosa L.
F. religiosa L.
F. semicordata Buch.-Ham.ex Sm.
Morus macroura Miq.
Streblus asper Lour.

MYRSINACEAE
Ardisia solanacea Roxb.
Maesa chisia Buch.-Ham. ex D. Don

MYRTACEAE
Cleistocalyx operculatus (Roxb.) Merr. & Perry
Eucalyptus sp.
Psidium guajava L.
Syzigium cumini (L.) Skeels.
S. operculatus (Roxb.) Merr.

OLEACEAE
Jasminum officianale L.
J. multiflorum (Burm.f.) Andrews & B. Repos.

ONAGRACEAE
Ludwiga hyssopifolia (G. Don) Exell
L. octavalvis (Jacq.) Raven

OROBANCHACEAE
Orobanche aegyptica Pers.

OXALIDACEAE
Oxalis corniculata L.

PAPAVERACEAE
Argemone mexicana L.

PIPERACEAE
Peperomia pellucidia (L.) Kunth
Piper nepalense Miq.

POLYGALACEAE
Polygala abyssinica R. Br.
P. crotalarioides Buch.-Ham. ex DC
P. longifolia Poiret

POLYGONACEAE
Persicaria barbata (L.) Hara
P. glabra (Willd.) Hara
P. hydropiper (L.) Spach.
Polygonum plebeium R. Br.

PRIMULACEAE
Anagallis arvensis L.

RANUNCULACEAE
Clematis gouriana Roxb.
C. grata Wall.
Ranunculus scleratus L.

RHAMNACEAE
Rhamnus nepalensis (Wall.) Lawson
Zizyphus incurva Roxb.
Z. mauritiana Lam.
Z. rugosa Lam.

RUBIACEAE
Adina cordifolia (Willd. ex Roxb.) Benth & Hook.
Anthocephalus chinensis (Lam.) A. Rich ex Wolp.
Coffea benghalensis Heyne ex Roem. & Shult.
Eriobotrya japonica Lindl.
Hedyotis lineata (Roxb.)
Hymenodictoyon excelsum (Roxb.) Wall.
Knoxia corymbosa Willd.
Mitragyna parviflorum (Roxb.) Korth.
Mussaenda frondosa L.
M. macrophylla Wall.
Randia tetrasperma (Roxb.) Benth.& Hook. ex Brandis.
Wendlandia exserta (Roxb.) DC.
W. tinctoria (Roxb.) DC.
Xeromphis spinosa (Thunb.) Keay
X. uliginosa (Retz.) Maheswari

RUTACEAE
Aegle marmelos (L.) Correa.
Chadleos paniculata L.
Citrus medica L.
Clausena pentaphylla DC.
Micromelum integerrium (Buch.-Ham.) Wight & Arn.
M. pubescens Hook.F.
Murraya koenigii Spreng.

SABIACEAE
Meliosma simplicifola (Roxb.) Walp.

SAPINDACEAE
Nephelium litchi Camb.
Schleichera oleosa (Lour.) Oken

SAPOTACEAE
Aesandra butyraceae Roxb.
Madhuca longifolia (Koenig.) MacBride

SAURAUIACEAE
Saurauria napaulensis DC.

SCROPHULARIACEAE
Lindenbergia indica (L.) Vatke
Lindernia antipoda (L.)
L. ciliata (Colsm.) Pen.
Scoparia dulcis L.
Vandellia ciliata (Colason) Yamazaki

SOLANACEAE
Physalis minima L.
Solanum anguivi Lam.
S. nigrum L.
S. surattense Burm. F.
S. torvum SW.

SONNERATIACEAE
Duabanga grandiflora (Roxb.) Walp.

STERCULIACEAE
Helicteres isora L.
Sterculia villosa Roxb.

TAMARICACEAE
Tamarix dioica Roxb.
T. indica Willd.

THEACEAE
Schima wallichii (DC.) Korthals.

TILIACEAE
Corchorus aestuans L.
Grewia hainesiana Hole.
G. helicterifolia Wall.
G. sapida Roxb. ex DC. Prod.
G. sclerophylla Roxb. ex G. Don
G. subinaequalis DC.
Triumfetta rhomboides Jacq.

ULMACEAE
Holoptela integrifolia (Roxb.) Planch.

UMBELLIFERAE
Oenanthe javanica (Bl.) DC.

Selinum tenuifolium Wall.ex C.B. Clarke
S. candollii DC.

URTICACEAE
Boehmeria macrophylla D. Don
B. rugulosa Wedd.
B. ternifolia D.Don
Girardinia diversifoila (Link) Friis et al.
Gonostegia pentandra (Roxb.) Miq.
Urtica dioica L.

VERBENACEAE
Callicarpa macrophylla Vahl.
Caryopteris odorata (D.Don) B.L. Robinson
Clerodendrum indicum (L.) Kuntze
C. viscosum Vent.
Gmelina arborea L.
Lantana camara L.
Lippia nodiflora (L.) Rich.
Premna obtusifolia R. Br.
Tectona grandis L.

VITACEAE
Leea compactiflora Kurz.
L. macrophylla Roxb.ex Hormen
Parthenocissus semichordata Wall. Planch
Tetrastigma serrulatum (Roxb.) Planch

Appendix iii

A checklist of birds recorded in the Royal Chitwan National Park up to 1988

KEY

Rating (in Chitwan)	*Habitat*	*Status*
1 = rare	f = forest	PM = Passage migrant
2 = less rare	g = grassland	R = Resident
3 = occasional	l = lakes/tals	S = Summer visitor
4 = fairly common	m = marshes	Sp = Spring visitor
5 = common	oc = open country	V = Vagrant
6 = very common	pb = Park boundaries	W = Winter visitor
	r = rivers	
	rf = riverine forest	
	sf = sal forest	
	w = near water	

NB. English names used, and their order here, are derived from *Birds of Nepal* by Fleming, Fleming and Bangdel. Scientific names follow those used in *A Guide to the Birds of Nepal* by C. and T. Inskipp.

	Rating	Habitat	Status
GREBES (PODICIPEDIDAE)			
Great crested grebe *Podiceps cristatus*	1	l	W
Little grebe *Tachybaptus ruficollis*	1-2	l & r	W/PM
CORMORANTS AND DARTER (PHALACROCORACIDAE)			
Large cormorant *Phalacrocorax carbo*	5	r	W
Little cormorant *Phalacrocorax niger*	2	l	W
Darter *Anhinga melanogaster*	5	l & r	R
HERONS AND BITTERNS (ARDEIDAE)			
Grey heron *Ardea cinerea*	4	m & r	W
Purple heron *Ardea purpurea*	4	m & r	mainly W some R
Little green heron *Butorides striatus*	4	l & r	R
Pond heron *Ardeola grayii*	6	m,l,r	R
Night heron *Nycticorax nycticorax*	5	l	R
Cattle egret *Bubulcus ibis*	4	pb	R
Large egret *Egretta alba*	4	r,m,l	R
Intermediate egret *Egretta intermedia*	4	m,r	R
Little egret *Egretta garzetta*	5	m,r	R
Chestnut bittern *Ixobrychus cinnamomeus*	3	g,m	R
Yellow bittern *Ixobrychus sinensis*	2	g,m	S
Black bittern *Dupetor flavicollis*	1	l edges	V
Eurasian bittern *Botaurus stellaris*	1	l edges	W/PM
STORKS (CICONIIDAE)			
Painted stork *Mycteria leucocephalus*	1-2	r	S
Open-billed stork *Anastomus oscitans*	5	g,m,l	R
White-necked stork *Ciconia episcopus*	3	g,l,r,m	R
White stork *Ciconia ciconia*	1	l,r	PM
Black stork *Ciconia nigra*	4	r	W
Black-necked stork *Ephippiorhynchus asiaticus*	2	r	W
Lesser adjutant stork *Leptoptilos javanicus*	3	m,r	R
CRANES (GRUIDAE)			
Common crane *Grus grus*	4	r	W
Sarus crane *Grus antigone*	1	pb	V
Demoiselle crane *Anthropoides virgo*	4	r	PM
IBISES (THRESKIORNITHIDAE)			
Black ibis *Pseudibis papillosa*	5	r	R
GEESE AND DUCKS (ANATIDAE)			
Bean goose *Anser fabalis*	1		V
Greylag goose *Anser anser*	1	r	W
Barheaded goose *Anser indicus*	2	r	W
Whistling swan *Cygnus columbianus*	1	r	V
Lesser whistling teal *Dendrocygna javanica*	5	m,l,r	R
Ruddy shelduck *Tadorna ferruginea*	6	r	W
Eurasian (or common) shelduck *Tadorna tadorna*	1		W/PM
Pintail *Anas acuta*	3	l,r	W

Common teal *Anas crecca*	4	l,r	W
Garganey *Anas querquedula*	1	r	PM
Spotbill duck *Anas poecilorhyncha*	1–2	l,r	W
Mallard *Anas platyrhynchos*	2	r	W
Gadwall *Anas strepera*	2	r	W
Falcated teal *Anas falcata*	1	l,r	W
Eurasian wigeon *Anas penelope*	2	r	PM
Shoveler *Anas clypeata*	2	r	W or PM
Red-crested pochard *Netta rufina*	2	r	W
Common pochard *Aythya ferina*	2	l,r	W
White-eyed pochard *Aythya nyroca*	1	r	PM
Tufted duck *Aythya fuligula*	2	r	PM
Cotton teal *Nettapus coromandelianus*	2	l	W
Goldeneye duck *Bucephala clangula*	1	l,r	W
Smew *Mergus albellus*	1	r	V
Merganser *Mergus merganser*	5	r	W

KITES, HAWKS, EAGLES AND VULTURES (ACCIPITRIDAE)

Black-crested baza *Aviceda leuphotes*	1	rf	S
Black-shouldered kite *Elanus caeruleus*	3	rf,g	R
Crested honey kite *Pernis ptilorhyncus*	5	sf,rf	R
Dark kite *Milvus migrans*	5	pb	W
Brahminy kite *Haliastur indus*	1	oc	W
Goshawk *Accipiter gentilis*	1–2	g,oc,f	W
Crested goshawk *Accipiter trivirgatus*	2	sf,rf	W
Sparrow hawk *Accipter nisus*	1		W?
Besra sparrow hawk *Accipiter virgatus*	1	sf,rf	W
Shikra *Accipiter badius*	4	sf,rf	R
Long-legged buteo *Buteo rufinus*	1		W
Eurasian buteo *Buteo buteo*	1	oc	W
White-eyed hawk *Butastur teesa*	4	g,rf	R
Crested serpent eagle *Spilornis cheela*	5	sf,rf	R
Short-toed eagle *Circaetus gallicus*	2	oc	W?PM?
Mountain hawk eagle *Spizaetus nipalensis*	2	sf	W
Changeable hawk eagle *Spizaetus limnaeetus*	2	sf,rf	R
Rufous-bellied hawk eagle *Lophotriorchis kienerii*	1	sf,rf	R?
Booted eagle *Hieraaetus pennatus*	2	sf,rf	W
Tawny eagle *Aquila rapax*	2	rf,oc	W
Steppe eagle *Aquila nipalensis*	2	rf,g	W
Greater spotted eagle *Aquila clanga*	1	rf,w	W
Imperial eagle *Aquila heliaca*	2		W?PM?
Lesser spotted eagle *Aquila pomarina*	2	rf,g,oc	W
White-tailed sea eagle *Haliaeetus albicilla*	2	f,w	W
Pallas's fishing eagle *Haliaeetus leucoryphus*	1	f,w	W
Black eagle *Ictinaetus malayensis*	1	g,sf	W
Grey-headed fishing eagle *Icthyophaga icthyaetus*	2	f,w	R
Himalayan grey-headed fishing eagle *Icthyophaga nana*	1	f,w	R
Black vulture *Torgos calvus*	2	sf,oc	W

Cinereous vulture *Aegypius monachus*	1	sf,oc	W
Eurasian griffon *Gyps fulvus*	4	sf,oc	W
Indian griffon *Gyps indicus*	4	sf,oc	R
White-backed vulture *Gyps bengalensis*	5	f,oc	R
Egyptian vulture *Neophron percnopterus*	3	oc,pb	W
Hen harrier *Circus cyaneus*	3	rf,g,m	W
Pale harrier *Circus macrourus*	1	g,oc	W
Montagu's harrier *Circus pygargus*	1	g,oc,w	PM
Pied harrier *Circus melanoleucus*	2	g,oc,w	W
Marsh harrier *Circus aeruginosus*	4	g,m,r	W
Osprey *Pandion haliaetus*	4	r,l,m	W

FALCONS (FALCONIDAE)

Red-thighed falconet *Microhierax caerulescens*	1	f,g	PM
Laggar falcon *Falco jugger*	1	oc	R?,PM?
Shaheen falcon *Falco peregrinus peregrinator*	1	sf,rf	W
Oriental hobby *Falco severus*	1	sf,rf	W
Eurasian hobby *Falco subbuteo*	1	f,g	W
Red-headed merlin *Falco chicquera*	1	fr,g	W?
Red-legged falcon *Falco amurensis*	1	oc	PM
Lesser kestrel *Falco naumanni*	1	g,oc	PM
Eurasian kestrel *Falco tinnunculus*	1–2	g,oc	W

PARTRIDGES, QUAIL AND PHEASANTS (PHASIANIDAE)

Black partridge *Francolinus francolinus*	4	g	R
Common or grey quail *Coturnix coturnix*	4	g	R?
Blue-breasted quail *Coturnix chinensis*	1	g,sf	R
Kalij pheasant *Lophura leucomelana*	3	sf	R
Common peafowl *Pavo cristatus*	5	g,rf	R
Red jungle fowl *Gallus gallus*	5	sf,rf/g	R

BUSTARD-QUAIL (TURNICIDAE)

Button quail *Turnix tanki*	4	g	R
Little bustard-quail *Turnix sylvatica*	3	g	R
Common bustard-quail *Turnix suscitator*	5	g	R

RAILS, CRAKES AND GALLINULES (RALLIDAE)

Baillon's crake *Porzana pusilla*	1	m,l	W
Ruddy crake *Porzana fusca*	3–4	m,l	R
Brown crake *Amaurornis akool*	5	m,l	R
White-breasted waterhen *Amaurornis phoenicurus*	5	m,l	R
Indian gallinule *Gallinula chloropus*	6	m,l	W
Purple gallinule *Porphyrio porphyrio*	3	l	W
Coot *Fulica atra*	1–2	l	W

BUSTARDS (OTIDIDAE)

Bengal florican *Houbaropsis bengalensis*	3	g	R/S
Lesser florican *Sypheotides indica*	1	g/oc	R?S?

JACANAS (JACANIDAE)

Pheasant-tailed jacana *Hydrophasianus chirurgus*	1	m,l	S
Bronze-winged jacana *Metopidius indicus*	4	m,l	R

WADERS (CHARADRIIDAE)

Red-wattled lapwing *Hoplopterus indicus*	5	r	R
Spur-winged lapwing *Hoplopterus duvaucelii*	5	r	R
Eurasian lapwing *Vanellus vanellus*	1	r	W
Yellow-wattled lapwing *Hoplopterus malabaricus*	1	r,pb	W
Grey-headed lapwing *Hoplopterus cinereus*	1	r	V
Eastern golden plover *Pluvialis dominica*	1-2	r,pb	PM
Little ringed plover *Charadrius dubius*	5	r	R
Kentish plover *Charadrius alexandrinus*	3	r	W
Lesser sand plover *Charadrius mongolus*	1	r	V
Whimbrel *Numenius phaeopus*	1	r	PM
Curlew *Numenius arquata*	1	r	PM
Common redshank *Tringa totanus*	2	r	W
Spotted redshank *Tringa erythropus*	1-2	r	W
Greenshank *Tringa nebularia*	6	r	W
Marsh sandpiper *Tringa stagnatilus*	1	r	W
Green sandpiper *Tringa ochropus*	5	r	W
Wood sandpiper *Tringa glareola*	3	r	W
Common sandpiper *Actitis hypoleucos*	5	r	W
Temminck's stint *Calidris temminckii*	5	r	W
Little stint *Calidris minuta*	1	r	V
Curlew sandpiper *Calidris ferruginea*	1	r	W/PM
Dunlin *Calidris alpina*	2	r	W/PM
Ruff *Philomachus pugnax*	1	m	W/PM
Jack snipe *Lymnocryptes minimus*	1	m	W?PM?
Pintail snipe *Gallinago stenura*	1	r	W
Fantail snipe *Gallinago gallinago*	3	r	W
Eurasian woodcock *Scolopax rusticola*	1		W

PAINTED SNIPE (ROSTRATULIDAE)

Painted snipe *Rostratula benghalensis*	2	l,m	R

AVOCETS AND ALLIES (RECURVIROSTRIDAE)

Black-winged stilt *Himantopus himantopus*	1	m,r	W
Pied avocet *Recurvirostra avosetta*	1	m	V

STONE PLOVERS (BURHINIDAE)

Eurasian thick knee *Burhinus oedicnemus*	4	r	R
Great thick knee *Esacus recurvirostris*	3	r	R

COURSERS AND PRATINCOLES (GLAREOLIDAE)

Small pratincole *Glareola lactea*	6	r	R
Oriental pratincole *Glareola maldivarum*	1	r	V

GULLS AND TERNS (LARIDAE)

Herring gull *Larus argentatus*	1	r	PM
Great black-headed gull *Larus ichthyaetus*	4	r	W
Black-headed gull *Larus ridibundus*	3	r	W
Brown-headed gull *Larus brunnicephalus*	1-2	r	W
Caspian tern *Sterna caspia*	1	r	W

Indian river tern *Sterna aurantia*	4	r	R
Common tern *Sterna hirundo*	1	l,r	PM
Black-bellied tern *Sterna acuticauda*	5	l,r	R
Little tern *Sterna albifrons*	4	r	S
Gull-billed tern *Gelochelidon nilotica*	1	r	V
Whiskered tern *Chlidonias hybridus*	1	r	V
White-winged black tern *Chlidonias leucopterus*	1	r	V

PIGEONS AND DOVES (COLUMBIDAE)

Pintail green pigeon *Treron apicauda*	1	sf	R
Thick-billed green pigeon *Treron curvirostra*	1	sf,rf	R
Orange-breasted green pigeon *Treron bicincta*	5	sf,rf	R
Grey-fronted green pigeon *Treron pompadora*	5	sf,rf	R
Bengal green pigeon *Treron phoenicoptera*	4	sf,rf	R
Imperial pigeon *Ducula badia*	1	rf	R?
Blue rock pigeon *Columba livia*	4	w	R
Rufous turtle dove *Streptopelia orientalis*	3	sf,rf	W
Red turtle dove *Streptopelia tranquebarica*	3	sf,rf	R
Indian ring dove *Streptopelia decaocto*	3	sf,rf,g	R
Little brown dove *Streptopelia senegalensis*	1	f	PM
Spotted dove *Streptopelia chinensis*	6	sf,rf,g	R
Emerald dove *Chalcophaps indica*	4	sf,rf	R

PARAKEETS (PSITTACIDAE)

Rose-ringed parakeet *Psittacula krameri*	6	sf,rf	R
Large parakeet *Psittacula eupatria*	5	sf,rf	R
Rose-breasted parakeet *Psittacula alexandri*	6	sf,rf	Rp
Blossom-headed parakeet *Psittacula cyanocephala*	4	sf,rf	R
Slaty-headed parakeet *Psittacula himalayana*	1	sf,rf	W
Indian lorikeet *Loriculus vernalis*	1	sf,rf	R?

CUCKOOS (CUCULIDAE)

Pied crested cuckoo *Clamator jacobinus*	2	sf,rf	S
Red-winged crested cuckoo *Clamator coromandus*	3	sf,rf	S
Large hawk cuckoo *Hierococcyx sparverioides*	1	rf	PM
Common hawk cuckoo *Hierococcyx varius*	5	rf	S
Eurasian cuckoo *Cuculus canorus*	3	sf,rf	S
Indian cuckoo *Cuculus micropterus*	4	rf	S
Banded bay cuckoo *Cacomantis sonneratii*	2	sf,rf	S
Plaintive cuckoo *Cacomantis merulinus*	2	sf,rf	S
Emerald cuckoo *Chrysococcyx maculatus*	1	rf	PM
Drongo cuckoo *Surniculis lugubris*	5	sf,rf	S
Large green-billed malkoha *Phoenicophaeus tristis*	3	sf,rf	R
Koel cuckoo *Eudynamys scolopacea*	2	sf,rf	S
Sirkeer cuckoo *Phoenicophaeus leschenaultii*	1	sf,rf	R?
Small coucal *Centropus toulou*	4	g	R
Large coucal *Centropus sinensis*	5	g	R

OWLS (STRIGIDAE)

Grass owl *Tyto capensis*	2	g	R

Scops owl *Otus sunia*	5	sf,rf	R
Collared scops owl *Otus bakkamoena*	2	sf,rf	R
Forest eagle owl *Bubo nipalensis*	2	sf,rf	R
Dusky horned owl *Bubo coromandus*	1	f	R
Tawny fish owl *Ketupa flavipes*	1	sf	R
Brown fish owl *Ketupa zeylonensis*	2	sf,w	R
Barred owlet *Glaucidium cuculoides*	4	sf,rf	R
Jungle owlet *Glaucidium radiatum*	5	sf,rf	R
Spotted owlet *Athene brama*	2	sf/rf,g	R
Brown hawk owl *Ninox scutulata*	4	sf,rf	R
Short-eared owl *Asio flammeus*	1		W?
NIGHTJARS (CAPRIMULGIDAE)			
Long-tailed nightjar *Caprimulgus macrurus*	4	sf/rf,g	S?
Jungle nightjar *Caprimulgus indicus*	4	sf	PM?
Little nightjar *Caprimulgus asiaticus*	1	f	S?
Franklin's nightjar *Caprimulgus affinis*	4	f/g,r	S
TROGONS (TROGONIDAE)			
Red-headed trogon *Harpactes erythrocephalus*	2	sf	R?
ROLLERS (CORACIIDAE)			
Dark roller *Eurystomus orientalis*	5	sf,rf	S
Indian roller *Coracias benghalensis*	5	sf,rf	R
HOOPOE (UPUPIDAE)			
Hoopoe *Upupa epops*	4	rf,g	R?
KINGFISHERS (ALCEDINIDAE)			
Small pied kingfisher *Ceryle rudis*	5	r	R
Large pied kingfisher *Ceryle lugubris*	1	r	V
Eurasian kingfisher *Alcedo atthis*	4	r,l	R
Blue-eared kingfisher *Alcedo meninting*	2	sf/w	R
Stork-billed kingfisher *Pelargopsis capensis*	3	r,l	R
White-breasted kingfisher *Halcyon smyrnensis*	5	r,l	R
Black-capped kingfisher *Halcyon pileata*	1	r	V
BEE-EATERS (MEROPIDAE)			
Chestnut-headed bee-eater *Merops leschenaulti*	6	rf/g,sf	S?
Blue-tailed bee-eater *Merops philippinus*	4	rf/g/w	S
Green bee-eater *Merops orientalis*	5	rf/g	S/R?
Blue-bearded bee-eater *Nyctyornis athertoni*	2	rf/g,sf	R
HORNBILLS (BUCEROTIDAE)			
Grey hornbill *Tockus birostris*	1	sf,rf	R
Pied hornbill *Anthracoceros coronatus*	4	sf,rf	R
Giant hornbill *Buceros bicornis*	3	sf,rf	R
BARBETS (CAPITONIDAE)			
Lineated barbet *Megalaima lineata*	5	sf,rf	R
Blue-throated barbet *Megalaima asiatica*	3	sf,rf	R
Crimson-breasted barbet *Megalaima haemacephala*	2	sf,rf	R

WOODPECKERS (PICIDAE)

Wryneck *Jynx torquilla*	2	rf/g	W
Rufous piculet *Sasia ochracea*	1	sf	R
Spotted piculet *Picumnus innominatus*	1	sf	R
Grey-crowned pigmy woodpecker *Dendrocopus canicapillus*	5	rf,sf	R
Brown-crowned pigmy woodpecker *Dendrocopus moluccensis*	1	rf	V
Fulvous-breasted pied woodpecker *Dendrocopus macei*	4	sf,rf	R
Yellow-fronted pied woodpecker *Dendrocopus mahrattensis*	1	rf	R
Small scaly-bellied woodpecker *Picus myrmecophoneus*	4	rf,sf	R
Black-naped woodpecker *Picus canus*	4	rf,sf	R
Large yellow-naped woodpecker *Picus flavinucha*	3	sf,rf	R
Small yellow-naped woodpecker *Picus chlorolophus*	4	sf,rf	R
Lesser golden-backed woodpecker *Dinopium benghalense*	3	sf	R
Three-toed golden-backed woodpecker *Dinopium shorii*	5	sf,rf	R
Large golden-backed woodpecker *Chrysocolaptes lucidus*	4	sf,rf	R
Brown woodpecker *Celeus brachyurus*	2	sf,rf	R
Great slaty woodpecker *Mulleripicus pulverulentus*	1	sf	R

BROADBILLS (EURYLAIMIDAE)

Long-tailed broadbill *Psarisomus dalhousiae*	1	sf,w	R?

PITTAS (PITTIDAE)

Indian pitta *Pitta brachyura*	5	sf,rf	S
Green-breasted pitta *Pitta sordida*	5	sf,rf	S

LARKS (ALAUDIDAE)

Bush lark *Mirafra assamica*	4	short g/r	R
Ashy-crowned finch lark *Eremopterix grisea*	1	r	R
Sand lark *Calandrella raytal*	5	r	R
Short-toed lark *Calandrella brachydactyla*	1	short g/oc	W?PM?

SWIFTS (APODIDAE)

Himalayan swiftlet *Collacalia brevirostris*	1		PM
White-rumped needletail *Zoonavena sylvatica)*	2	f,g	R?
Large white-rumped swift *Apus pacificus*	1	g/w	W?
House swift *Apus affinis*	1	g,f	R?
Alpine swift *Apus melba*	3	f,g	R?
Crested swift *Hemiprocne longipennis*	5	f,g	R
Asian palm swift *Cypsiurus balasiensis*	1	PM	
White-vented needletail *Hirundapas cochinchinensis*	1	r	R?
White-throated needletail *Hirundapas caudacuta*	1	r,g	PM

SWALLOWS AND MARTINS (HIRUNDINIDAE)

Collared sand martin *Riparia riparia*	1		V
Sand martin *Riparia paludicola*	6	r	R
Barn swallow *Hirundo rustica*	4	oc	R
Striated swallow *Hirundo daurica*	4	oc	R?
Nepal house martin *Delichon nipalensis*	1	r,f	W
Asian house martin *Delichon dasypus*	1		V
Common house martin *Delichon urbica*	1		V

SHRIKES (LANIIDAE)

Bay-backed shrike *Lanius vittatus*	1	f,g	V
Black-headed shrike *Lanius schach*	3	rf,g	R
Grey-backed shrike *Lanius tephronotus*	1	f	W,V
Brown shrike *Lanius cristatus*	1	g/rf	W

ORIOLES (ORIOLIDAE)

Golden oriole *Oriolus oriolus*	5	rf,sf	S
Black-naped oriole *Oriolus chinensis*	1	rf,sf	W?
Black-headed oriole *Oriolus xanthornus*	6	rf,sf	R
Maroon oriole *Oriolus traillii*	1	sf	W/·V

DRONGOS (DICRURIDAE)

White-bellied drongo *Dicrurus caerulescens*	4	sf,rf	R
Small racquet-tailed drongo *Dicrurus remifer*	3	sf	R?W?
Large racquet-tailed drongo *Dicrurus paradiseus*	3	sf	R
Hair-crested drongo *Dicrurus hottentottus*	4	sf	R
Ashy drongo *Dicrurus leucophaeus*	4	sf,rf	R?S?
Black drongo *Dicrurus macrocercus*	4	rf/g,sf	R
Little bronzed drongo *Dicrurus aeneus*	5	sf,rf	R
Crow-billed drongo *Dicrurus annectans*	5	sf,rf,g	R

WOOD SWALLOWS (ARTAMIDAE)

Ashy wood swallow *Artamus fuscus*	4	sf,rf	R

STARLINGS AND MYNAS (STURNIDAE)

Spot-winged stare *Saroglossa spiloptera*	4	rf	S
Brahminy myna *Sturnus pagodarum*	1	rf	R?
Grey-headed myna *Sturnus malabaricus*	4	rf,sf	R?S?
Eurasian starling *Sturnus vulgaris*	1	pb	PM
Pied myna *Sturnus contra*	3	pb	R
Common myna *Acridotheres tristis*	3	rf/g,sf	R
Bank myna *Acridotheres ginginianus*	3-4	r	R
Jungle myna *Acridotheres fuscus*	6	sf,rf,g	R
Talking myna *Gracula religiosa*	3-4	sf,rf	R

CROWS AND ALLIES (CORVIDAE)

Green magpie *Cissa chinensis*	2	sf,rf	R
Red-billed blue magpie *Urocissa erythrorhyncha*	3	sf	R
Indian tree-pie *Dendrocitta vagabunda*	4	sf,rf	R
Jungle crow *Corvus macrorhynchos*	5	sf,rf	R
House crow *Corvus splendens*	1	pb	R

MINIVETS AND ALLIES (CAMPEPHAGIDAE)

Lesser wood-shrike *Tephrodornis pondicerianus*	4	sf,rf	R
Large wood-shrike *Tephrodornis gularis*	4	sf,rf	R
Pied wood-shrike *Hemipus picatus*	5	sf,rf	R
Large cuckoo-shrike *Coracina novaehollandiae*	5	sf,rf	R
Dark cuckoo-shrike *Coracina melaschistos*	2-3	sf,rf	R?
Black-headed cuckoo-shrike *Coracina melanoptera*	1	f	PM
Long-tailed minivet *Pericrocotus ethologus*	2	sf,rf	W
Scarlet minivet *Pericrocotus flammeus*	5	sf,rf	R
Rosy minivet *Pericrocotus roseus*	4	sf,rf	R?S?
Small minivet *Pericrocotus cinnamomeus*	3	sf,rf	R

LEAF BIRDS AND ALLIES (IRENIDAE)

Iora *Aegithina tiphia*	5	sf,rf	R
Golden-fronted leaf bird *Chloropsis aurifrons*	4	sf,rf	R
Orange-bellied leaf bird *Chloropsis hardwickii*	2	sf,rf	R

BULBULS (PYCNONOTIDAE)

Black-headed yellow bulbul *Pycnonotus melanicterus*	3-4	sf,rf	R
Red-whiskered bulbul *Pycnonotus jocosus*	6	sf,rf,g	R
White-cheeked bulbul *Pycnonotus leucogenys*	3	sf,rf	R
Red-vented bulbul *Pycnonotus cafer*	6	sf/rf/g	R
White-throated bulbul *Criniger flaveolus*	1	sf,rf	V
Grey bulbul *Hypsipetes madagascariensis*	3	sf,rf	R

BABBLERS, LAUGHING-THRUSHES AND ALLIES (TIMALIIDAE)

Spotted babbler *Pellorneum ruficeps*	5	sf,rf	R
Slaty-headed scimitar babbler *Pomatorhinus schisticeps*	3	sf,rf	R
Rusty-cheeked scimitar babbler *Pomatorhinus erythrogenys*	2	sf,rf	R
Lesser scaly-breasted wren babbler *Pnoepyga pusilla*	1-2	sf,rf/w	W?
Yellow-breasted babbler *Macronous gularis*	5	sf,rf	R
Black-chinned babbler *Stachyris pyrrhops*	5	sf,rf	R
Black-throated babbler *Stachyris nigriceps*	4	sf,rf	R
Rufous-bellied babbler *Dumetia hyperythra*	1	sf	R?
Yellow-eyed babbler *Chrysomma sinense*	4	rf/g	R
Red-capped babbler *Timalia pileata*	5	rf/sf/g	R
Jungle babbler *Turdoides striatus*	4	sf/rf/g	R
Striated babbler *Turdoides earlei*	5	g	R
Slender-billed babbler *Turdoides longirostris*	3	g	R
Lesser necklaced laughing-thrush *Garrulax monileger*	3	sf,rf	R
Large necklaced laughing-thrush *Garrulax pectoralis*	4	sf	R
Rufous-necked laughing-thrush *Garrulax ruficollis*	4	rf/sf/g	R
White-bellied yuhina *Yuhina zantholeuca*	4	sf,rf	R
Nepal babbler *Alcippe nipalensis*	2	sf,rf	R

FLYCATCHERS (MUSCICAPIDAE)

Sooty flycatcher *Muscicapa sibirica*	1-2	sf,rf	PM

Brown flycatcher *Muscicapa latirostris*	1	rf/g	PM
Rufous-tailed flycatcher *Muscicapa ruficauda*	1	sf,rf	PM
Red-breasted flycatcher *Muscicapa parva*	3	sf,rf	W
Verditer flycatcher *Muscicapa thalassina*	2	sf,rf	W
Brooks' flycatcher *Muscicapa poliogenys*	5	sf,rf	R
Orange-gorgetted flycatcher *Ficedula strophiata*	1	rf	W
Little pied flycatcher *Ficedula westermanni*	2	sf,rf	W
Slaty blue flycatcher *Ficedula leucomelanura*	1	rf/g,sf	W
Rufous-breasted blue flycatcher *Ficedula hyperythra*	1	sf,rf	W
Rusty-breasted blue flycatcher *Ficedula hodgsonii*	1	sf,rf	W
White-throated blue flycatcher *Ficedula superciliaris*	1		PM
Kashmir redbreasted flycatcher *Ficedula subrubra*	1		PM
Blue-throated flycatcher *Cyornis rubeculoides*	1	sf,rf	W
Tickell's blue flycatcher *Cyornis tickelliae*	1		?
Black-naped flycatcher *Hypothymis azurea*	3	sf,rf	R?S?
Paradise flycatcher *Terpsiphone paradisi*	5	sf,rf	S
White-throated fantail flycatcher *Rhipidura albicollis*	5	sf,rf	R
White-breasted fantail flycatcher *Rhipidura aureola*	3	sf,rf	R
Yellow-bellied fantail flycatcher *Rhipidura hypoxantha*	1		W
Grey-headed flycatcher *Culicicapa ceylonensis*	4	sf,rf	R

WARBLERS (SYLVIIDAE)

Slaty-bellied ground warbler *Tesia cyaniventer*	1	sf,rf	W
Chestnut-headed ground warbler *Tesia castaneocoronata*	1	sf,rf	W
Blanford's bush warbler *Cettia pallidipes*	3–4	sf/g	R
Aberrant bush warbler *Cettia flavolivacea*	1	rf/g,sf	W
Large bush warbler *Cettia major*	1	g	W
Rufous-capped bush warbler *Cettia brunnifrons*	2	g	W
Spotted bush warbler *Bradypterus thoracicus*	1	g	W
Golden-headed cisticola *Cisticola exilis*	2	g	R
Zitting cisticola *Cisticola juncidis*	3	g	R?
Hodgson's prinia *Prinia hodgsonii*	4	sf/rf/g	R
Grey-capped prinia *Prinia cinereocapilla*	4	sf/rf/g	R
Plain prinia *Prinia inornata*	2	g,sf/g	R
Ashy prinia *Prinia socialis*	3	sf/rf/g	R
Yellow-bellied prinia *Prinia flaviventris*	4	g	R
Fulvous-streaked prinia *Prinia gracilis*	1	g	R?
Brown hill prinia *Prinia criniger*	2	sf	R?W
Large grass warbler *Graminicola bengalensis*	3	g	R
Bristled grass warbler *Chaetornis striatus*	1	g	S?
Tailor bird *Orthotomus sutorius*	5	sf,rf	R
Streaked grasshopper warbler *Locustella lanceolata*	1	g	W
Striated marsh warbler *Megalurus palustris*	1	g/w	R
Clamorous or great reed warbler *Acrocephalus stentoreus*	1–2	g/m	W
Thick-billed warbler *Acrocephalus aedon*	1	g	W

Booted warbler *Hippolais caligata*	1		V
Orphean warbler *Sylvia hortensis*	1		V
Blyth's reed warbler *Acrocephalus dumetorum*	3	rf/g	W?,PM?
Paddyfield warbler *Acrocephalus agricola*	1–2	g/m	W
Lesser whitethroat *Sylvia curruca*	1	f	W?
Brown leaf warbler *Phylloscopus collybita*	4	rf,sf	W
Tickell's leaf warbler *Phylloscopus affinis*	2	rf,sf	W
Smoky leaf warbler *Phylloscopus fuligiventer*	1	rf/g	W?PM
Dusky leaf warbler *Phylloscopus fuscatus*	1	rf/g	W?PM
Dull leaf warbler *Phylloscopus trochiloides*	4	rf,sf	W
Large-billed leaf warbler *Phylloscopus magnirostris*	1	rf	W
Plain leaf warbler *Phylloscopus inornatus*	3	rf,sf	W
Yellow-rumped leaf warbler *Phylloscopus proregulus*	3	rf,sf	W
Crowned leaf warbler *Phylloscopus reguloides*	5	rf,sf	W
Large crowned leaf warbler *Phylloscopus occipitalis*	5	rf,sf	W
Green warbler *Phylloscopus nitidus*	1		PM
Olivaceous leaf warbler *Phylloscopus griseolus*	1		V
Yellow-eyed warbler *Seicercus burkii*	4	rf,sf	W
Grey-headed warbler *Seicercus xanthoschistos*	3	rf,sf	W
Chestnut-crowned warbler *Seicercus poligenys*	2	rf,sf	W
Yellow-bellied warbler *Abroscopus superciliaris*	2	rf,sf	W

THRUSHES, CHATS AND ALLIES (TURDIDAE)

White-browed shortwing *Brachypteryx montana*	1	rf	W?
Himalayan rubythroat *Luscinia pectoralis*	1	mg/g/f	W?
Eurasian rubythroat *Luscinia calliope*	1	g/rf	W
Bluethroat *Luscinia svecica*	1	m/g	W
Blue chat *Luscinia brunnea*	1	sf,rf	PM
Shama *Copsychus malabaricus*	5	sf,rf	R
Robin dayal *Copsychus saularis*	5	sf,rf	S
White-tailed blue robin *Cinclidium leucurum*	1	sf/w	W?
Black redstart *Phoenicurus ochruros*	3	g	W
White-capped river chat *Chaimarrornis leucocephalus*	1	r/f	W
Plumbeous redstart *Rhyacornis fuliginosus*	2	r	W
Black-backed forktail *Enicurus immaculatus*	4	sf/w	R
Collared bush chat *Saxicola torquata*	5	g	R
White-tailed bush chat *Saxicola leucura*	4	g	R
Dark-grey bush chat *Saxicola ferrea*	1–2	g	W?
Pied bush chat *Saxicola caprata*	5	g	R
Hodgson's bush chat *Saxicola insignis*	1	g/w	V
Blue rock thrush *Monticola solitarius*	2	r	W
Desert wheatear *Oenanthe deserti*	1	r	V
Northern wheatear *Oenanthe oenanthe*	1		V
Blue-capped rock thrush *Monticola cinclorhyncha*	1	f	PM
Indian robin *Saxicoloides fulicata*	1–2	rf/pb	R
Orange-headed ground thrush *Zoothera citrina*	5	sf,rf	S
Speckled mountain thrush *Zoothera dauma*	1	w/sf/rf	W

Large long-billed thrush *Zoothera monticola*	1	sf/w	W
Grey-winged blackbird *Turdus boulboul*	2	sf,rf	W
Tickell's thrush *Turdus unicolor*	1	sf,rf	W/PM?
Black-throated thrush *Turdus ruficollis*	5	rf	Sp/PM
Whistling thrush *Myiophoneus caeruleus*	3	sf/w	R

TITMICE (PARIDAE)

Grey tit *Parus major*	5	sf,rf	R

NUTHATCHES (SITTIDAE)

Chestnut-bellied nuthatch *Sitta castanea*	5	sf,rf	R
Velvet-fronted nuthatch *Sitta frontalis*	5	sf,rf	R
Wall creeper *Tichodroma muraria*	2	r,w	W

PIPITS AND WAGTAILS (MOTACILLIDAE)

Hodgson's tree pipit *Anthus hodgsoni*	5	sf,rf	W
Paddyfield pipit *Anthus novaeseelandiae rufulus*	5	g	R
Richard's pipit *Anthus novaeseelandiae richardi*	2	g	W
Rose-breasted pipit *Anthus roseatus*	2–3	w	W
Eurasian tree pipit *Anthus trivialis*	1	rf/g	W
Tawny pipit *Anthus campestris*	1		V
Red-throated pipit *Anthus cervinus*	1	pb	V
Water pipit *Anthus spinoletta*	1	m	V
Forest wagtail *Dendranthonus indicus*	1	f	V
Yellow wagtail *Motacilla flava*	4	w	W
Grey wagtail *Motacilla cinerea*	4	w	W
Yellow-headed wagtail *Motacilla citreola*	4	w	W
Pied wagtail *Motacilla alba*	5	r	W
Large pied wagtail *Motacilla maderaspatensis*	5	r	R

FLOWERPECKERS (DICAEIDAE)

Thick-billed flowerpecker *Dicaeum agile*	1	sf	W?
Tickell's flowerpecker *Dicaeum erythrorhynchos*	3	sf,rf	R
Fire-breasted flowerpecker *Dicaeum ignipectus*	1	sf	W?
Plain flowerpecker *Dicaeum concolor*	1		?

SUNBIRDS (NECTARINIIDAE)

Scarlet-breasted sunbird *Aethopyga siparaja*	3	sf,rf	R
Black-breasted sunbird *Aethopyga saturata*	1		PM
Rubycheek *Anthreptes singalensis*	1	sf,rf	R
Purple sunbird *Nectarinia asiatica*	4	sf,rf	R?
Little spiderhunter *Arachnothera longirostra*	1	sf/w	R
Streaked spiderhunter *Arachnothera magna*	3	sf,rf	R?

WHITE-EYE (ZOSTEROPIDAE)

White-eye *Zosterops palpebrosa*	6	sf,rf	R

SPARROWS AND WEAVER BIRDS (PLOCEIDAE)

House sparrow *Passer domesticus*	3	pb	R
Yellow-throated sparrow *Petronia xanthocollis*	3	rf/sf	R
Black-throated weaver *Ploceus benghalensis*	4	g	R
Baya weaver *Ploceus philippinus*	5	g	R

Red munia *Amandava amandava*	3	g	R
Sharp-tailed munia *Lonchura striata*	3	rf/g/sf	R
Spotted munia *Lonchura punctulata*	5	sf/g	R
Black-headed munia *Lonchura malacca*	4	g	R

FINCHES (FRINGILLIDAE)

Common rose finch *Carpodacus erythrinus*	4	rf	Sp/PM

BUNTINGS (EMBERIZIDAE)

Red-headed bunting *Emberiza bruniceps*	1	pb	V
Yellow-breasted bunting *Emberiza aureola*	3	g/pb	W
Black-faced bunting *Emberiza spodocephala*	1	g	PM
Grey-headed bunting *Emberiza fucata*	1	g	W
Rustic bunting *Emberiza rustica*	1		V
Crested bunting *Melophus lathami*	3	f/g	W?

Appendix iv

A checklist of butterflies recorded in the Royal Chitwan National Park

* Commonly seen species.

ACRAEIDAE
Yellow coster *Acraea issoria*

AMATHUSIIDAE
Common duffer *Discophora sondaica*

DANAIDAE
Plain tiger* *Danaus chrysippus*
Common tiger* *D. genutia*
Blue glassy tiger* *Tirmala limniace*
Dark blue tiger *T. septentrionis*
Glassy tiger* *Parantica aglea*
Chocolate tiger *Danaus melaneus*
Common Indian crow* *Euploea core*
Magpie crow *E. diocletianus*
Striped blue crow* *E. mulciber*

HESPERIIDAE
Common small flat *Sarangesa dasahara*
Dusky yellow-breasted flat *Daimio phisara*
Indian skipper* *Spialia galba*
Restricted demon *Notocrypta curvifascia*
Grass demon* *Udaspes folus*
Palm red-eye *Erionata thrax*
Common grass dart *Taractrocera maevius*
Indian dart *Potanthus pseudomaesa*

Contiguous swift *Polytremis lubricans*
Contiguous swift* *Pelopidas sinensis*
Small branded swift *P. matthias*
Bengal swift *P. agna*
Bevan's swift *Barbo bevani*
Spotted angle *Caprona agama f. agama*
Bush hopper *Ampittia dioscorides*
Dingy scrub hopper *Aeromachus dubius*
Purple and gold flitter *Zographetus satwa*
Common red-eye *Matapa aria*
Ceylon dartlet *Oriens goloides*

LYCAENIDAE
Common gem *Poritia hewitsoni*
Apefly *Spalgis epius*
Silverstreak blue *Iraota timoleon*
Indian oakblue *Arhopala atrax*
Large oakblue *A. amantes*
Centaur oakblue *A. centaurus*
Dark himalayan oakblue *A. rama*
Falcate oakblue *Mahathala ameria*
Common acacia blue *Surendra vivarna*
Red spot *Zesius chrysomallus*
Fluffy tit *Zeltus amasa*
Orchid tit *Chliaria othona*
Yamfly *Loxura atymnus*
Common onyx *Horaga onyx*
Slate flash *Rapala manea*
Common flash *R. pheritima*
Indigo flash *R. varuna*
Common silverlines *Spindasis vulcanus*
Angled sunbeam *Curetis acuta*
Indian sunbeam *Curetis thetis*
Banded lineblue *Prosotas lutea*
Common lineblue* *P. nora*
Ciliate blue *Anthene emolus*
Peablue* *Lampides boeticus*
Forget-me-not blue *Catochrysops strabo*
Metallic cerulean *Jamides alecto*
Common cerulean* *J. celeno*
Common pierrot* *Castalius rosimon*
Spotted pierrot *Tarucus callinara*
Gram blue *Euchrysops cnejus*
Lesser grass blue *Zizina otis*
Tiny grass blue *Zizula hylax*
Dark grass blue* *Zizeeria karsandra*
Pale grass blue* *Z. maha*
Lime blue *Chilades lajus*
Common hedge blue *Acytolepsis puspa*
Malayan *Megisba malaya*
Grass jewel *Freyeria trochilus*

NEMEOBIIDAE
Plum judy *Abisara echerius*
Plum judy *A. bifasciata*
Punchinello* *Zemeros flegyas*

NYMPHALIDAE
Indian fritillary* *Argyreus hyperbius*
Common leopard* *Phalanta phalantha*
Vagrant *Vagrens egista*
Rustic* *Cupha erymanthis*
Blue admiral* *Kamiska canace*
Indian red admiral* *Vanessa indica*
Painted lady* *V. cardui*
Indian tortoiseshell* *Aglais cashmirensis*
Angled castor* *Ariadne ariadne*
Common castor* *A. merione*
Yellow pansy* *Precis hierta*
Blue pansy* *P. orithya*
Lemon pansy* *P. lemonias*
Grey pansy* *P. atlites*
Chocolate pansy* *P. iphita*
Peacock pansy* *P. almana*
Danaid eggfly *Hypolimnas misippus*
Great eggfly* *H. bolina*
Orange oakleaf *Kallima inachus*
Commander *Limenitis procris*
Colour sergeant *Athyma nefte*
Common sergeant* *A. perius*
Staff sergeant *A. selenophora*
Common lascar* *Pantoporia hordonia*
Clear sailer *Neptis clinia*
Common sailer* *N. hylas*
Burmese sailer *N. nata*
Sullied sailer *N. soma*
Short-banded sailer *Phaedyma columella*
Common baron* *Euthalia aconthea*
Common earl *Tanaecia julii*
Grey count* *T. lepidea*
Common map* *Cyrestis thyodamas*
Tawny rajah *Charaxes polyxena*
Red lacewing *Cethosia biblis*
Tabby* *Pseudergolis wedah*
Painted courtesan *Euripus consimilis*
Common nawab *Polyura athamus*

PAPILIONIDAE
Tailed jay *Graphium agamemnon*
Glassy bluebottle *G. cloanthus*
Common jay *G. doson*
Common bluebottle* *G. sarpedon*
Spot swordtail *Pathysa nomius*

Common mime* *Chilasa clytia*
Common mormon* *Papilio polytes*
Red helen *P. helenus*
Great mormon* *P. memnon*
Lime swallowtail* *P. demoleus*
Paris peacock *P. paris*
Common rose* *Pachliopta aristolochiae*
Common birdwing *Troides helena*
Rose windmill *Atrophaneura latreillei*

PIERIDAE
Large cabbage white* *Pieris brassicae*
Indian cabbage white* *P. canidia*
Bath white *Pontia daplidice*
Yellow orange tip* *Ixias pyrene*
Common jezebel *Delias eucharis*
Painted jezebel *D. hyparete*
Red-base jezebel *D. pasithoe*
Psyche *Leptosia nina*
Great orange tip *Hebomoia glaucippe*
Common wanderer *Valeria valeria*
Common emigrant* *Catopsilia pomona f. crocale*
Lemon emigrant* *C. pomona f. pomona*
Mottled emigrant* *C. pyranthe*
Three-spot grass yellow* *Terias blanda*
Common (or two-spot) grass yellow* *T. hecabe*
Small grass yellow *T. brigitta*
Pioneer *Belenois aurota*
Common gull* *Cepora nerissa*
Dark clouded yellow *Colias fieldii*

SATYRIDAE
Common evening brown* *Melanitis leda*
Treebrown* *Lethe confusa*
Bamboo treebrown *L. europa*
Common palmfly *Elymnias hypermnestra*
Blind-eye bushbrown* *Mycalesis mamerta*
Dark-brand bushbrown* *M. mineus*
Common bushbrown* *M. perseus*
Jungle brown* *Orsotrioena medus*
Common five-ring *Ypthima baldus*
Common four-ring *Y. huebneri*
Common four-ring *Y. kasmira*
Large three-ring *Y. nareda*
Newar three-ring *Y. newara*

Further Reading

Anderson, Mary M. *Festivals of Nepal*. Allen and Unwin, London, 1971.

APA Productions (Hk) Ltd. *Insight Nepal*. Fifth edition, Hong Kong, 1986.

APA Productions (Hk) Ltd. *Book of Indian Wildlife, Sri Lanka and Nepal*. Hong Kong, 1987.

Bell, Diana J. *A Study of the Biology and Conservation of the Hispid Hare*. School of Biological Sciences, University of East Anglia, UK, 1987.

Bista, D.B. *People of Nepal*. Kathmandu Dept. of Publicity, Nepal, 1976.

Bolton, M. *Royal Chitwan National Park Management Plan (1975-79)*. Project Working Document No.2 Nat. Parks and Wildlife Conservation Project, Kathmandu, Nepal, 1975.

Cubitt, Gerald and Mountfort, Guy. *Wild India — The Wildlife and Scenery of India and Nepal*. Collins, 1985.

Daniel, J.C. *Book of Indian Reptiles*. Bombay Natural History Society, Bombay, India, 1983.

De, R.C. and Spillett, J.J. "A Study of Chital or Spotted Deer in Corbett Nat. Park. Uttar Pradesh." *J. Bombay Nat. Hist. Soc.* 63:576-593, 1966.

Evans, M., *et al. Report of Edinburgh University Expedition to Nepal, Nov.1984 — Feb 1985*. "An ecological survey of the Narayani River within Royal Chitwan National Park. A study of the fish distribution and their predators, in particular the Smooth Indian Otter (*Lutra perspicillata*)."

Fleming, R.L. Jnr and R.L. Snr and Bangdel, Lain Singh. *Birds of Nepal*. Nature Himalayas, Box 229 Kathmandu, Nepal, 1976.

Gajurel, C.L. and Vaidya, K.K. *Traditional Arts and Crafts of Nepal*. S. Chand and Co. Ltd, Ram Nagar, New Delhi 110055, India, 1984.

Gurung, K.K. *Heart of the Jungle*. Andre Deutsch, London, 1983.

H.M.G. Dept of Medicinal Plants. *Wild Edible Plants of Nepal*. Thapathali, Kathmandu, Nepal, 1982.

Holloway, C.W., *et al. Conservation of the Tiger (Panthera tigris tigris L.) in India*. (World Wildlife Fund Report) 1976.

Inskipp, C. and T. *A Guide to the Birds of Nepal*. Croom Helm, London and Sydney, 1985.

Kailash — A Journal of Himalayan Studies. Vol VII 1979 Nos.4-3. Ratna Pustak Bhandar, Bhotahity, Kathmandu, Nepal.

Laurie, A. "*Ecology and Behaviour of the Greater One Horned Rhinoceros (Rhinoceros unicornis).*" Ph.D. Thesis. University of Cambridge, England, 1978.

Lehmkuhl, John. F., *et al. Grass and People in Royal Chitwan National Park: A survey of grass value and villager attitudes*. King Mahendra Trust for Nature Conservation, Box 3712, Kathmandu, Nepal, 1987.

Majupuria, T.C. *Wild is Beautiful*. S. Devi, Lalitpur Colony, Lashkar (Gwalior), M.P. India, 1982.

Manandhar, N.P. *Medicinal Plants of Nepal Himalaya*. Ratna Pustak Bhandar, Bhotahity, Kathmandu, Nepal, 1980.

McDougal, Charles. *Face of the Tiger*. Andre Deutsch, London, 1980.

Mierow, Dorothy and Shrestha, Tirtha Bahadur. *Himalayan Flowers and Trees*. Sahayogi Press, Tripureswor, Kathmandu, Nepal, 1978.

Milton, J.P. and Binney, G.A. *Ecological Planning in the Nepalese Terai: A Report on resolving resource conflicts between wildlife conservation and agricultural land use in Padampur Panchayat.* Threshold, International Centre for Environmental Renewal, Washington DC, USA, 1980.

McGladdery, S., *et al. Report of Aberdeen University Expedition to Nepal 1980.* "A survey of fish in rivers and lakes of Chitwan National Park.'

Mishra, H.R. "Ecology of the Chital (*Axis axis*) in Royal Chitwan National Park: With Comparisons with Hog Deer (*Axis porcinus*), Sambar (*Cervus unicolor*) and Barking Deer (*Muntiacus muntjak*)." Ph.D. dissertation, University of Edinburgh, UK, 1982.

Mishra, H.R. "Balancing Human Needs and Conservation in Nepal's Royal Chitwan Park." *Ambio* 11:246 — 52, 1982.

Mishra, H.R. and Mierow, D. *Wild Animals of Nepal.* Ratna Pustak Bhandar, Kathmandu, Nepal, 1974.

Mitchell, Joseph C. and Zug, George R. *Guide to the Amphibians and Reptiles of Royal Chitwan National Park.* Nat. Museum of Natural History, Smithsonian Institute, Washington DC.

Mountfort, G. *Saving the Tiger.* Viking Press, New York, USA, 1981.

Polunin, Oleg and Stainton, Adam. *Flowers of the Himalaya.* Oxford University Press, New Delhi, India, 1984.

Prater, S.H. *Book of Indian Animals.* Bombay Natural History Society, Bombay, India, 1971. Third ed.

Seidensticker, J.C. "On the Ecological Separation Between Tigers and Leopards." *Biotropica* 8: 225-34, 1976.

Seidensticker, J.C. "Ungulate Population in Chitwan Valley." Nepal. *Biological Conservation* 10:183-210, 1976.

Sharma, U. *A Study of Park People Interactions in Royal Chitwan National Park.* World Wildlife Fund, USA. 1986.

Shrestha, Tej Kumar. *Wildlife of Nepal.* Curriculum Development Centre, Tribhuvan University, Kathmandu, Nepal, 1981.

Smith, C.K. *Field Guide to Nepal's Butterflies.* Tribhuvan University Press, Tribhuvan University, Kathmandu, Nepal, 1981.

Smith, J.L.D. "Dispersal, Communications and Conservation Strategies for the Tiger (*Panthera tigris*) in Royal Chitwan National Park." Ph.D. Thesis, University of Minnesota, St Paul, USA, 1984.

Smith, J.L.D., *et al.* "Female Land Tenure System in Tigers." *Tigers of the World*, 11:97-109, Noyes Publications, 1987.

Stainton, A. *Flowers of the Himalaya — A Supplement.* Oxford University Press, Delhi, India, 1988.

Stainton, J.D. *Forests of Nepal.* John Murray, London, 1974.

Storrs, Adrian and Jimmie. *Discovering Trees in Nepal.* Sahayogi Press, Tripureswor, Kathmandu, Nepal, 1984.

Sunquist, M.E. "The movements and activities of Tigers (*Panthera tigris tigris*) in Royal Chitwan National Park." Ph.D. Thesis, University of Minnesota, St Paul, USA, 1979.

Sunquist, M.E. "The Social Organisation of Tigers (*Panthera tigris*) in Royal Chitwan National Park." Smithsonian Contrib. *Zool.* No. 336, 1981.

Tamang, K.M. "Population Characteristics of the Tiger and its Prey." Ph.D. Thesis, Michigan State University, East Lansing, USA, 1979.

Whitaker, R. *Common Indian Snakes; a Field Guide.* Macmillan Co. of India, New Delhi, India, 1978.